A Modern Girl's Guide to Getting Hitched

Sarah Ivens is the former Editor of *OK!* magazine and has previously written for *Tatler*, *Marie Claire*, *Hello!*, *GQ*, the *Observer*, the *Daily Mail* and the *Mirror*, Sarah is married and lives in East London.

Also by Sarah Ivens:

A Modern Girl's Guide to Dynamic Dating
A Modern Girl's Guide to Etiquette
A Modern Girl's Guide to Networking
A Bride's Guide to Unique Weddings
A Modern Girl's Guide to Getting Organised
A Modern Girl's Guide to Perfect Single Life
The Bride's Guide to Unique Weddings

A Modern Girl's Guide to Getting Hitched

*How to plan, survive and enjoy
your wedding*

S A R A H   I V E N S

piatkus

PIATKUS

First published in Great Britain in 2002 by Piatkus
Reprinted 2002 (twice), 2005 (twice), 2006 (twice),
2007, 2008, 2009 (twice), 2010 (twice), 2011

A CIP catalogue record for this book
is available from the British Library.

ISBN 978-0-7499-2268-9

Printed in the UK by CPI Mackays, Chatham ME5 8TD

Piatkus
An imprint of
Little, Brown Book Group
100 Victoria Embankment
London EC4Y 0DY

An Hachette UK Company
www.hachette.co.uk

www.piatkus.co.uk

Dedication

For my mother, who made me what I am, and my husband,
who loves me the way I am.

Contents

Introduction

A bride-to-be's life is not a simple one

It seems so easy. Boy meets girl. Girl meets boy. They fall in love. She realises after one week that she can't live without him and they should get married. He realises the same thing – but after a much longer period of time – and he drops down on one knee and asks the question. If it is true love (and we're assuming it is), she says yes and they get married. They live happily ever after. That's how it always happened at Disney.

The reality starts the same: they fall in love, he asks, she says yes – but stop right there. It's not as simple as just getting married. Anyone who says 'just get married' has obviously never even attempted to do such a thing. In fact, the most annoying thing about falling in love and getting engaged is that you have to organise the wedding.

You enjoy the romance of being a fiancée for about two months and then – wham – you're a bride-to-be with a mission. You will have the best wedding ever. You will be the most beautiful bride in the world. You will have a happy and successful marriage... and this is just what your mother is telling you. In truth, your main mission is to get through the whole process without killing your parents, having a nervous breakdown and conducting an escapist affair with a man in your office.

I got married in October 2000. The fifteen months prior to the day itself were a rollercoaster of fear, excitement, panic, dread, regret, poverty and shock. I was expected to spend a sickening amount of time thinking about distant relatives whom I have never liked, my preferences for icing over marzipan and the convenience of outside toilets. I turned into a monster; a wedding bore with an attitude problem, a Bridezilla with frequent paranoia attacks.

My main problem was that I thought I was the only one going through these irrational ups and downs. In the movies – and in wedding magazines – brides are perceived as sweet, gentle girls who look lovely all the time. I wanted to swear like a trooper and start smoking again. And as for looking lovely? The stress did nothing for my skin or my nails. This is where this book comes in. I hope that by sharing the hard facts and real dramas, you will be able to get on with planning the best day of your life without making the same mistakes I did. Try to enjoy every minute because, believe me, as soon as it's over, you'll have envy attacks every time you come across a modern girl with it all to look forward to.

When I was getting married, I wish I'd had an easy-to-use guidebook that told me the bare facts and explained the common misconceptions. Magazines are perfect for finding a dream dress but they can't explain bridal neurosis. I have written this book by recalling my bleakest moments and remembering what got me through them: the basic rules, advice from friends and amazing tips that I would never have thought of. So, along with a general guide to all the elements of your wedding and the run-up to it, I have also included anecdotes from countless past brides and their foolproof Secrets of Success. I've also devised an Ideal Time Planner, so that you can get organised from six months before the wedding until the day before.

Good luck... survive the next few months and you can survive anything!

Chapter One

Coming to terms with never being able to pull men again

No DOUBT, YOUR LIFE SO far has been awash with childhood crushes, teenage romances and twenty-something relationships. Now you have found the man of your dreams, what do you do? Marry him of course. It may be difficult to relinquish your dating techniques to your single sisters, but where you are going, you won't need them. You may have twinges of sadness that you will never be able to pull rugby players in nightclubs again, or even that you will never have to sit by the telephone for two weeks thinking, 'will he, won't he?' Yet if your man is special enough to marry, he is special enough to start staying in on a Saturday night for. So enjoy love, security and loyalty and shout '*Au revoir le* singledom' from the rooftops.

The proposal

As every woman knows (and every man should remember), a proposal isn't just about asking someone to marry you. It will come to signify your relationship forever more. So try to make sure it's worth repeating. Obviously, the girl isn't supposed to know anything about it. This is, after all, one of the man's only responsibilities during the whole wedding process before he backs off into a pre-matrimonial coma.

JANE, 30

❝ My husband is lovely: sweet, generous, honest, and hard working. That's why it is so sad that my proposal was such a disaster. Apparently he had planned to propose on a holiday later in the year, but during a particularly vicious bout of food poisoning, he thought he'd ask to cheer me up. I was in my sweaty pyjamas in bed. He burst in like a rabbit caught in headlights. He asked the question, I said yes, he tried to kiss me but it made me nauseous. He explained that he hadn't planned to propose this early so he didn't have the ring, but he had stopped off at the jewellers for some brochures. He was upset that I had ignored them, but I couldn't summon up the energy to sip water, let alone enthuse over pages of diamonds. ❞

Should he ask for your father's permission to marry you?

Tricky one. He won't want to. He's probably a bit scared of your dad and finds it difficult enough talking to him about the football scores. And anyway, maybe you'd be affronted that he was treating you like a possession swapped from man to man. Your dad would probably like to be asked, although nowadays, it does seem a bit sexist and ridiculous. Also, your dad might say no and put a damper on the whole thing.

As soon as you are engaged, decide what the best thing for everyone is. If you'd like your fiancé to talk to your father, remind him how close you are to your dad. If you feel strongly that it's got nothing to do with your dad, make this clear. It will save your partner a lot of unnecessary stress and sweat.

What to do if the dream proposal is a nightmare?

Grin and bear it. What else can you do? If this is the one for you, you can't really strop off and say, 'Not until you ask me properly!' But before you tell anyone else how it happened, change your state of mind and turn the negative into a positive. When anyone asks you how it happened, embellish the truth or act coy and let his or her imagination take over.

If he really hasn't made an effort at all, demand a second proposal and get him to take you to your favourite restaurant, hotel or – at a push – city to make up for it. This might be a fun thing to do a few months before the wedding.

The engagement ring

Traditionally, a man is supposed to spend the equivalent of one month's salary on the engagement ring. This takes a lot of saving, as he'll still have the bills to pay without looking suspiciously thrifty. If he's taken the effort to choose a ring for you, he loves you very much. Men don't like shopping at the best of times, so the fact that he spent time hanging about in jewellery shops speaks volumes. If he has chosen badly (or meanly), choose an extra-glam wedding band – or demand a diamond-encrusted eternity ring when you give birth to your first child.

To many of you, the thought of being presented with a ring is probably horrific. There is nothing wrong in choosing together, in fact, although less romantic, it might be more practical in the long run. You will get exactly what you want and he won't have to worry about disappointing you with his choice.

Telling the world your good news

The impact the engagement has will depend on how many people your fiancé has already told. In a whirl of excitement – and a certain degree of self-confidence – my husband told the world we were getting engaged before I'd said yes. This replaced the 'can you believe it?' factor with a house full of family and friends waving helium balloons when we returned from Rome, where he had proposed. This was fun – and saved on the phone calls – but I resented being such an open-and-shut case in the proposal stakes. Maybe he should have waited, just in case I'd said no. He won me over by describing what the last few months had been like for him (stressful, uncertain, expensive) and that to keep his morale high, he needed to double-check his plans with our nearest and dearest.

If you haven't told people yet, try not to do so via email or fax. Even to tell people over the phone is a shame, although, in some cases, inevitable. Where it's possible, tell family and friends when you are together as a couple – and near a stock of champagne, or at least sparkling wine. You'll be amazed by people's genuine joy and excitement... because after all, everyone loves a good wedding.

For pure drama and decadence, take out an advertisement in the local paper. This is a good way to show ex-classmates or colleagues that you are a rounded, wanted woman with a future ahead of her. For extra impact, add flamboyant details of the wedding and your great career. Exaggerate as necessary to get revenge on bitches from your past.

Engagement parties: the done thing or an added expense?

If you're a party person, you will feel completely justified in throwing a soirée in your own honour. Invite your friends and family over for a glass of champagne (or twelve), and an eyeful of your new piece of jewellery – if they decide to bring you a present, all the better. Don't assume you will receive engagement presents – most people consider a card sufficient – and certainly don't let your smile drop a mile when friends arrive on your doorstep with little more than a bottle of Chardonnay and an eighties compilation tape.

Traditionally, engagement parties have been used to introduce close friends and families on one side to their equivalent on the other. And alcohol always does make stressful situations like these a little easier, provided your guests know when to stop and don't suggest any naked Twister.

If you don't fancy a party, then don't bother. Soon you will have had your fill of balloons, music, drink and buffet food – you don't need to draw out the process. When weddings cost so much, as they do now, couples have to start saving from day one of the engagement. It's perfectly acceptable to celebrate with close friends and family at a restaurant and save the mad, bad party for the evening of the wedding.

Do we have to call each other fiancé/e?

The titles fiancé and fiancée leave you in a kind of no-man's-land: they are difficult to spell and no one can remember which one refers to the man and which one refers to the woman. If you've always wanted to be one, go for it. If not, stick to partner/boyfriend/lover. Try to avoid 'other half' at all costs – people will start wondering why you're not a whole person anymore.

Are you a complete commitment-phobe?

Your initial reaction is probably to say, 'No way, José – I accepted the ring, didn't I? And I maintained a pretty serious relationship before the rock was even a little twinkle in his eye.' Think again perhaps. Dating someone is a big deal; living with someone is a test and sharing a mortgage proves you're getting on very well. But marriage? That is the hard-core commitment test. Apart from having a child together, getting married is the single most drastic thing you can do to change your life irretrievably for one other person. This is why engagement – particularly in the first few months – throws up so many unwanted questions: do you want to be a Mrs? Do you want to be 'her indoors'? Do you want your loving boyfriend to start referring to you as his 'ball and chain'? And anyway, aren't you a bit too young for this? Surely you've got years ahead of you, why rush ahead now?

How will you act as an engaged woman?

In theory: engaged women carry a sense of contentment, maturity, and *joie de vivre*. They glow with the promise of a life-long love affair. They get giddy with excitement at the sight of a wedding magazine. They daydream all day long about their bridal hair and make-up and giggle with their friends about the 'first night' of marriage.

In reality: as an engaged woman you should expect to descend into madness relatively quickly. Weddings aren't fun to organise; they are expensive, stressful and time-consuming. You will cease to exist as a friend, colleague, and lover. You will become 'Bridal Woman'; a sort of super-hero who carries sugared almonds as bullets. You will strive to achieve perfection through adversity, depression and bouts of nausea.

Can you still be fun and young despite being married?

Admittedly, when a couple choose to settle down, buy a house and get married, their priorities change. Instead of challenging passing sailors to games of strip poker, you may now find your attention turned to fabric swatches and parquet flooring. This doesn't mean you've got old and dull; it's just that your interests have moved on. If you're determined to prove you can still be a young, crazy cat in the run up to your big day, encourage your girlfriends to join you at a local discotheque. Dance with the DJ, down ten pints of cider and spend hours wandering around the town looking for a kebab shop before finally collapsing on a street corner. You'll soon appreciate the new, more mature you.

JILL, 28

❝ I felt very panicky about getting married at 26 and in the months before my wedding reverted to my teenage self. I started smoking again, dug out all my old CDs and started moping around the house and reading love letters from my ex-boyfriend. I was obviously having some mid-twenties crisis. Getting married feels like a very grown-up thing to do. My mum says she still feels like a teenager now and gets a shock when she sees an older woman looking back at her in the mirror. Maybe people will always try to recapture their youth when the truth about growing old hits them. That would explain balding, middle-aged men wearing bad wigs. ❞

Secrets of Success...

◆ Parents should always be the first to hear of an engagement, except if you have children from a previous marriage. It will have a greater impact on your children than your parents.

◆ Traditional wedding guides include whole chapters on who you cannot get engaged to (your brother, father, grandfather, son, uncle or nephew). I will assume you know this already.

◆ Set the date as soon after the engagement as possible – things get booked up months in advance.

◆ If you want to go formal, the wording on a press announcement should be: Mr and Mrs John Smith, of Somewhere, are pleased to announce the engagement of their youngest /oldest/prettiest daughter, Doris, to John Bloggs, elder /youngest/ugliest son of Mr and Mrs Joe Bloggs, of Anywhere. Allow for text changes in event of death or divorce.

◆ An engagement ring is not a must, but it certainly doesn't hurt. Although diamonds are traditional, other precious stones can bring good luck at weddings. Emeralds signify hope, sapphires symbolise wisdom and rubies bring passion. If you get the option, pick a stone to suit your personality.

◆ If money is a problem, second-hand rings are a very attractive option. Look out for Victorian and Edwardian designs, which make a stunning change from the mass-produced designs of today.

◆ You could ask for your engagement ring to be engraved with the date of the proposal as a memento.

◆ It is traditional for the man to spend a month's salary on his fiancée's ring and it is a nice idea for the woman to buy him something special in return. Buy a keepsake, such as a pair of cufflinks, to celebrate.

♦ While you are choosing your engagement ring, remember that you will be wearing it with your wedding band. Don't choose a yellow-gold ring if you want a platinum band – and make sure they will fit neatly together.

♦ If you're famous or rich and live in America, a pre-nuptial agreement is handed over at the same time as the engagement ring but they are not legally binding in the UK. If you're both financially paranoid, they are fine for establishing intention and ownership and can be used as evidence in divorce courts. They can, however, be overturned by a court if they are inequitable and unfairly prejudice a party's position. Don't tell anyone you are even thinking of pre-nups – they'll judge your relationship and give unwanted advice.

♦ A 'tester' fling with an ex- is not a good idea. Neither is a mope over old pictures of your first boyfriend. The past is in the past. Leave it there. They must have been wrong for you or they wouldn't be yesterday's men.

Chapter Two

The big issues

BEFORE YOU CAN get carried away on a taffeta wave of minor details and decoration, you need to answer the big questions: when, where, how and how much? The most important thing to do is pick a date. Everything will follow. If you only have a month to plan your wedding, choices will be limited, so you should run like the wind to get your wedding sorted. If you have a little longer, you will have time to plan and save. 'Save' being the operative word.

Why are weddings so hideously expensive?

It would be great to say that the reason weddings are so expensive is because they are worth it, because it is important to throw all your money into one big day to celebrate your life and love together. Just remember, however, the wedding might be fun, but the marriage won't be if you get yourselves into debt for the sake of a few extra helium balloons. It's much more important for modern couples to get sorted before they go splashing their cash around. Try to clear student loans, get a deposit together for a house and make sure you've got job security. Weddings are only so hideously expensive because couples won't show any restraint – and also because florists, caterers, designers and stationers see you coming. They must recognise the post-engagement glow or something. Mention the word 'wedding' and the price for any goods or service doubles. If you fancy taking a risk, don't mention the 'w' word until you've got a quote in writing. It will be too late for them to pull a fast one by then.

Planning your budget

The first two questions you should ask yourself are:

◆ How many months do we have to save before the wedding?

◆ How big a wedding are we hoping to have?

As soon as you have answered these questions, you'll be able to sort out your expenses, which will lead you to the third most important question:

◆ How much can I spend on my dress?

Obviously, if your budget is minimal and the whole wedding party is going to consist of you, your man and two witnesses you've never met before, it might be inappropriate to blow the budget on your dress. You might come across as self-centred and vain. But if money really is no object, the bride should treat herself – go hell for leather for the perfect gown. More on this in Chapter Five.

Entertaining yourself on the cheap

Just because you are getting married it doesn't mean you have to become a social recluse until the big day. In fact the opposite is true. You don't want to spend so long saving and refusing to go out that you haven't got any friends left by the time the big day arrives. You must still go out, just don't go to casinos and five-star restaurants. Instead, invite friends round for a takeaway; start taking an interest in long country walks and orienteering; revisit your video collection with a bag of popcorn or throw wild parties where everyone brings a bottle (this normally replenishes your drinks cabinet).

Being treated like a charity case isn't so bad

During the build-up to your wedding, friends and family will assume you're short of cash and there will be a sympathetic flurry of dinner invitations. Don't feel bad that you can't repay the favour with a sumptuous banquet the following week. Your friends will be happy just to help you out, and you can repay them for the kindness at the wedding by making it a great day out. If friends offer to buy you theatre or concert tickets, don't reject them. Enjoy their generosity and make a mental note to take them out when the wedding is over.

How many people can I afford to invite?

It is a shame that your guest list will depend largely on how many people you can afford to invite, but you do need to be ruthless. You can't invite everyone. Here is a good rule: if you haven't seen them in the last year, chances are you won't see them in the next five either so don't invite them. Make special allowances for family and friends living overseas.

DONNA, 27

❝ I turned into a financial fascist when it came to saving. Although we set the date two years before, I made us save every penny. That meant no holidays, luxuries or nights out. We wasted our engagement being boring, and by the wedding we looked ill and stressed. I would also look at my friends in terms of cash, thinking, 'Are they worth that amount of money?' I practically had cartoon dollar signs flash up in my eyes when I knocked them off the guest list. ❞

Setting the scene

How to choose the right venue for you

Planning the reception (picking the venue, menu and entertainment) is the singularly most important and expensive aspect of the wedding. Choices can spiral out of control as couples comply with tradition, hiring rooms in an expensive hotel and providing plenty of food and drink for their guests. Holding the reception in a hotel is still the preferred choice – they provide space, facilities and experience. You book what you want and they will take care of the details, such as toastmaster, DJ and flowers. And the added bonus is they use people who feel comfortable with the venue and this reduces the chances of anything going wrong. There are a few key points to bear in mind:

◆ Do you want to hold the wedding near to where you live?

◆ Do you want the venue to be yours exclusively for the whole day?

◆ Do you want to cater for the event or do you want in-house caterers?

◆ Do you have enough funds to finance your ideal wedding location?

If you want to hold the reception in a hotel but are worried about costs, there are ways around it. Why not have a late ceremony and go straight into the evening reception, serving just a light buffet for guests? Or if you'd planned an earlier ceremony, follow with a refined cocktail reception with canapés, before leaving after a few hours to have a quiet dinner elsewhere with close family. You'll need to be strong-willed to push for these two options when everyone else is demanding 'a bit of a do' but it's your wedding and it's your wallet that's being hit from all sides.

If you are looking into using an expensive hotel to host your wedding, it's good to know that if you consider getting married on a weekday, venues will often negotiate cheaper rates for you. This may make your expensive dream an affordable reality.

JANE, 31

❝ Getting married on a Friday did save us a substantial amount of money – but remember, parents might not want to take their children out of school for the day and many people will not be able to take the day off work. Nearly a quarter of our guests couldn't make it, which is a real shame. ❞

If you have a favourite restaurant or even a nightclub, what about holding the party there? You could have an intimate meal with close friends and family directly after the service, and then go on to meet the others – if you do hold it in a nightclub, arrange a group booking for discounted entrance fees. This will cost you, but it will still be cheaper than a traditional reception.

It often seems like a good idea to host the reception in a local school hall or community centre. You will need to do a lot more of the arranging in this case, including getting a food and alcohol licence from the local council. It is more work, but you have more control, and it is a lot cheaper.

For the same reasons – and with the same organisational hassles – you could have a wedding at home, or at your parent's home. Just prepare yourself with good catering staff that supplies crockery, glasses and a mobile bar – and think about car parking. Hire a marquee and/or mobile toilets if you are worried about space and amenities. You should also bear in mind that you or your parents will find lots of drunken revellers in their lounge/garage/vegetable patch the next day. Think about the time of year as well. Your house may be able to hold 100 people when the weather is nice and they can spill out into the garden. What would it be like in the rain?

Anything is possible: you can get married in a castle, on a beach, on a boat, in a football ground, theme park or mountain range. If scenery and atmosphere are more important to you than cutting the costs and ease, go with your dream. Lots of people will think you are silly, flash or helplessly modern, but it's your wedding day and the worst thing would be going for the safe option of a hotel's banqueting suite and regretting it for the rest of your life.

If you have to think about your budget when choosing where to get married, look into getting married abroad. That way, the few guests who do attend will pay for themselves and you will not have the added expense of hiring a venue and caterers: the resort will sort out a package for you.

Jo, 32

❝ I wanted to get married in the house I was brought up in, so I managed to persuade my parents to erect a marquee in their garden and host the event. They weren't at all keen but I explained what it would mean to me and how special it would make the day for all the guests. In the end, all it meant was lots of vomit on their driveway, trampled flowerbeds, a ruined carpet and lots of washing up for us all to do the next day. ❞

Food

You may love goat's cheese, grilled Dover sole and passion fruit but chances are your guests have more simple tastes (which is no bad thing where costs are involved). When you are catering for a large number of people, you have to go for the popular choice of menu which is generally soup or melon to start, followed by chicken or salmon, and rounded off with chocolate cake. By the time guests finally get to eat they will be starving so will be happy if the food is warm and served in good portions. Always offer good variations for vegetarians and children. Perhaps put a note on the invitations about dietary requirements. Again, think about the time of year – on a hot summer's day, guests won't be thrilled to be greeted by a hot and spicy soup and a roast dinner.

Catering for your needs

♦ A sit-down meal with waiters will allow guests to relax while the food is brought to them but the service may be slow and haphazard. Eat at the venue before you book, to check the standards.

♦ A sit-down buffet allows guests to choose their own food and quantities and then return to the calmness of their set table. Make sure there are two buffet tables to keep queues to a minimum.

♦ A stand-up buffet can allow guests to choose their own menu and then to mingle with whomever they choose. Make sure there are plenty of chairs for those who wish to sit down and also provide some tables for drinks and empty plates.

The evening buffet is a must if you expect guests to keep dancing and dancing for hours after the sit-down meal. Offer a good selection of hot and cold snacks – sandwiches, pizza slices and crisps are always the most popular options. Don't go mad on the order though – most buffets are half left at the end of the night so don't let the venue staff convince you to order one buffet order per person. One between two is plenty.

If food isn't a monetary priority, have a late wedding and go straight into the party. This cuts out the expensive wedding breakfast, the traditional name for a wedding meal, and many people prefer buffets where they can help themselves anyway. If it is summer, barbecues are simple, quick, cheap and unusual.

Drink

At some weddings, drink is the most important factor in making it a success. I went to a fantastic wedding where the bride's father left bottles of port on each table to go with the cheese and biscuits, and then followed with bottles of brandy to accompany the coffee. Needless to say, the DJ didn't have any trouble getting people on the dance-floor... he just had trouble getting them off it at the end of the night. People like a drink to let their hair down and loosen their inhibitions, but it is expensive. As a rule, supply half a bottle of wine per person during the meal, and one glass of champagne or fizzy wine for the toasts. What you do before and after depends on you and your budget. My dad had fantasised about making it a free bar all night at my wedding. My husband and I talked him out of it by convincing him of the wastage, spillage and foolishness of certain friends. Thank God he listened. In the end, he paid for a free bar for one hour before the meal, and the bill came to over £2,000.

Before you book a venue, check drink prices and packages. They can vary a great deal. Some hotels will offer wine with the meal for a set price, which works out cheaper. Other hotels will exploit their captive market with inflated bar prices, which may leave guests feeling disgruntled. Also ask the venue how long they are allowed to serve alcohol for. You don't want to book the DJ to play until 1.00 a.m. for the bar to shut at 11.00 p.m.

If money is tight, hold the reception at a venue where you can take your own alcohol. It's amazing how pre-dinner drinks, wine with dinner and champagne for the toasts add up. Save money buying in bulk from a warehouse or, if you are living in the UK, going to France. Remember, you don't have to serve expensive wine or champagne either. Another cost cutter is to serve fun, cheap cocktails like Pimms or sangria. Before you do, make sure the venue has a bring-your-own licence and that they don't charge extortionate corkage. Some venues charge so much that it works out more expensive to bring your own alcohol.

Secrets of Success

◆ Decide when to have the wedding, thinking about seasonal pros and cons like the weather and public holidays. Although summer is the best time for sunshine, bear in mind that many guests will be unable to attend as they are on holiday. A winter wedding may be atmospheric but snow can cause problems.

◆ As soon as you can, sit down and make a list of all of your costs, deposits paid and the final payment due date. This will help you mentally prepare for the expense.

◆ If you can't trust yourselves to keep enough cash aside, open a new wedding bank account and set up standing orders to take cash from your current account on pay day.

◆ Don't moan to your friends about the costs too much. You've chosen to get married and invited everyone you've ever met. If you whine too much, your friends will feel too guilty to enjoy the day as your guests.

◆ Don't hint to your boss that you deserve a pay rise. Pay rises are given for hard work, promotion and new skills – not for getting married and spending more than you earn.

◆ Take out wedding insurance. For a minimal cost, it will save you paying out twice if anything goes wrong.

◆ Keep it in perspective. It might be worth taking out an over-draft if it means you can have a dream honeymoon. A controllable debt will be paid off before the memories fade.

◆ Find out, as soon as you can, if your parents are going to contribute. This will halt any misunderstandings and resentment. If they don't want to give you a set sum, ask them to pay for a certain thing, such as the flowers, which is within their price range.

◆ People will want to buy you wedding presents. If money is looking tight, how about asking close family to contribute towards your bouquet, dress or honeymoon as a gift instead of something from a list.

◆ Speak to as many ex-brides as you can. They have been through it all and may have picked up some great, reasonable contacts on the way. And don't forget that you are the customer and you are spending your hard-earned cash on the wedding. If a supplier isn't up to scratch, look for another.

◆ Understand that many businesses cannot offer final prices a long time before the date, so remain flexible. Always budget for a little more than the estimate.

◆ If you're that worried about saving, take out a loan, convert to the Greek Orthodox Church and ask wedding guests to pin bank notes to your gown until it is completely covered. This is a charming custom that allows couples to have the wedding they want without panicking about paying for it. In a way, the guests pay to enjoy themselves so everyone's a winner.

◆ Always get three quotes for every wedding service or product you need and don't be afraid to tell the suppliers that you are looking around and doing your research. Don't necessarily pick the cheapest option. The middle price is more likely to be competitive and reliable.

◆ For a cheap-and-easy wedding breakfast, choose a theme and then hold the reception at an appropriate local restaurant, such as Italian, Greek or Indian. Normal restaurant prices will be more reasonable than inflated wedding catering.

◆ Spice up the buffet with unusual options. Some couples set up sweet stalls at the same time, to please guests with a sweet tooth, and stock up on childhood favourites. Another popular treat is to have a fish trolley. One of the catering staff goes around the guests offering fresh oysters, smoked salmon canapés and crab puffs. Just make sure it is all fresh – you don't want to poison your nearest and dearest. Other options include fish and chips, Italian-themed buffets with pizza and pasta, and an ice cream stall.

◆ Always remember to serve plenty of water and soft drinks at the reception for the hot, the sensible, the under eighteens and the designated drivers.

◆ Although it is traditional to serve red wine with red meat and white wine with fish and poultry, most people prefer white wine, so serve three bottles of white to every two of red – or you will have lots of red left over and lots of empty glasses.

◆ Use the Ideal time planner (*see* page 179) to chart your progress.

Chapter Three

The finishing touches

PLANNING THE VENUE and the menu may take all the time and money, but when it comes to making your wedding original and memorable, it is the finer points that matter.

The real PMT

Forget your period, your real troubles as a woman start when you say 'yes' and your mother starts making 'arrangements'. Those crazy American 'life experts' will tell you not to sweat the small stuff. Don't believe them. Never underestimate the impact that attention to small details will make. You may panic that you are spending an unhealthy amount of time analysing the consistency of a fruitcake, but it's worth it. What would happen if the wedding cake was so tough your Granny's false teeth got stuck in it and she had to spend the rest of the reception toothless? It wouldn't be pretty, and that's just one thing that could go wrong. You are right to develop a finely tuned sense of paranoia, anxiety and fear over the specific details of your wedding. You may develop a string of nasty skin disorders, terrifying mood swings and stomach pains, but hopefully they'll diminish by the big day, if not the honeymoon. This is purely Pre-Marriage Tension.

Stationery to get you going

Traditionally sent by the bride's mother if the bride's parents are hosting the event, the invitations should be sent out three months before the day. If you and your partner are paying for the wedding, you can choose who the invitations should be addressed from – either yourselves or your parents, or both sets of parents. All invitations should be sent out at the same time so that guests do not assume they are second choice. The groom's parents and all attendants should also receive invitations.

Style

The invitations should reflect the couple and the style/theme of the wedding. From informal to very formal, from glittery to flowery, the guests should get some indication of what's going to happen on the day. For a very small, informal wedding you can send all guests hand-written letters telling them about the wedding.

How many do you need?

If you are ordering a set of invitations, allow one invitation per couple or per family. Always order at least ten more than you need to allow for mistakes when writing out names and addresses. If you are getting them printed, ask to see a proof before they go ahead and produce a large number – even if you have clearly explained wording and spellings, mistakes will creep in. Ask someone else to proof-read them for you too.

While you are ordering invitations, think about ordering menu cards, orders of service, the seating plan and place cards. This will save time, perhaps money, and will continue the same colours and themes.

What should we say on the invitation?

The wording should be clear, free from ambiguity and state exactly who is invited. Don't write 'Jane, John and family' and then sulk if they show up with all their children and children's girl/boyfriends. If you don't want to invite children to the wedding, don't leave any room for misunderstandings on the invite. It sounds daft, but make sure you put the time and address of the wedding on the invitation – many couples forget.

If you are hosting the wedding, the invitation should state 'Jane Bride and David Groom request the pleasure of your company at their marriage at...' If your parents are hosting the wedding, the invitation should state 'Mr and Mrs John Bride request the pleasure of the company of... at the marriage of their daughter Jane to Mr David Groom at ...' If your parents are divorced but hosting the wedding together, the invite should state 'Mr John Bride and Mrs Helen Bride request the pleasure of the company of... at the marriage of their daughter Jane to Mr David Groom at...'

Flower power

Along with the dress, flowers should be a choice personal to the bride. The size and colour will depend on your dress, and therefore so do the bridesmaid's posies. As well as personal choice, think of the flowers' staying power (they may have to sit in the church or reception for up to 24 hours) and the time of year. You may want to have orchids in December, but importing them at that time of year may push you over budget. Florists will advise you on price and availability to get you on the right track. Designs are usually chosen from illustrated catalogues – or the bride can give the florist a photograph or sketch of her dream design and they can work from that. It may also help to take a picture of your dress to the florist for inspiration. Even if you don't know what you want straight away, find a florist that suits you and book them early. Give them the date of your wedding so that they can allot time to your needs. As long as you give them your final choice a month before the day, they will be able to get everything you need.

While you are designing your bouquets, think about sprays and buttonholes. If you do not want the whole congregation to wear buttonholes, just provide them for the fathers and attendants. Sprays should be ordered for both mothers and any other special people, such as sisters and grandmothers. Speak to the florist about ideas for the venues such as pew decoration, table centrepieces and pedestals, although the church and/or venue may have in-house people who will be able to prepare flowers for less money.

It is sometimes possible to cut costs at venues by sharing the flower bill with another couple getting married on the same day. Ask the venue to put you in touch with other couples.

What do different flowers symbolise?

Before you go ahead and order a bouquet, check that the flowers don't represent anything too sinister or are associated with funerals and death. You may just see a pretty flower but older relatives will grimace with fear.

Good flowers: daffodil (respect), daisy (innocence), forget-me-not (true love), ivy (good luck), orchid (beauty), pansy (thoughtfulness), white rose (charm), tulip (love).

Bad flowers: arum lily (death), larkspur (fickleness), narcissus (egotism), yellow rose (envy).

Art of decoration

The traditional wedding uses flowers to decorate the rooms where the bride, groom and guests spend any time. But flowers are incredibly expensive so look for other fun, alternatives to make a visually stunning wedding; perhaps using ribbon and ivy wrapped around pillars and doors to bring a country feel inside. Use ribbon in the same colour as the bridesmaid dresses to tie everything into a theme. Candles look stunning – especially at winter weddings – so place these carefully on windowsills, in fireplaces and on tables. For added effect, sprinkle tables and surfaces with glitter and foil stars to catch the light. Draping fairy or chilli lights around the venue is another way of adding a magical feel for very little money. A fun, original gimmick I saw at a wedding once was a picture wall. The bride and groom made copies of all their favourite pictures of themselves, friends and family, and decorated the walls of the venue with them – it was a great conversation piece and everyone felt included in their special day. Balloons and streamers can add quick, cheap and easy appeal to a room – especially when used in the wedding colours. Some people may think they're tacky and induce helium-fuelled singsongs, but they are big and bright which is great for large venues. Think about getting some banners designed – and either make them yourself or go to a local printer – with your names and the date of your wedding on. If you want fresh flowers, make one big display rather than lots of little ones and put them somewhere prominent like the entrance hall or next to the top table.

DANIELLE, 28

❝ We loved the idea of making the wedding more like a party than a formal event. Instead of flower displays, we sprinkled the room with sequins and erected a huge net over the dance-floor, filled with balloons. When everyone joined us after the first dance, we asked the DJ to play party seventies music; the balloons tumbled down and the waitresses handed out streamers, whistles and tambourines. At midnight, we finished off the day with a firework display and gave everyone sparklers. Our guests loved the originality. ❞

Rings of truth

The giving of rings is an ancient custom, symbolising complete, never-ending love – the eternal circle. It was traditional to give diamond engagement rings and plain gold bands from the 15th century until the 18th century when the 'love ring' – with two hands clasping a heart – became a fashionable alternative. Today, the couple can choose whatever they like. Decide if you both would like matching rings, and if yours must match your engagement ring, and then visit as many different jewellers as possible until you see something you like at a good price. It is worth avoiding the high-street chain stores, which charge high prices, and looking instead for a designer or jewellery warehouse. You'll find the quality of metal is identical but they do not have huge overheads. If you want the rings to be designed

Birthstones and their meanings

Month	Birthstone	Meaning
January	garnet	constancy
February	amethyst	sincerity
March	bloodstone	courage
April	diamond	innocence
May	emerald	success
June	pearl	purity
July	ruby	love
August	sardonyx	married bliss
September	sapphire	wisdom
October	opal	hope
November	topaz	fidelity
December	turquoise	harmony

especially for you, or engraved with your names or the date, leave plenty of time. Make sure you try on the rings before the day as well. Your hands will be shaky enough during the vows – you don't want the rings to be too small or too big as well!

Remember, don't worry if you haven't got the money to get your dream, diamond-encrusted band for the wedding – there's always the eternity ring he owes you when you give birth to your first child.

Driving power

As long as it gets you to the church on time, you don't care what it is. Or so you thought. Maybe now that you have the dream dress, dream bouquet and a gaggle of stunning bridesmaids, you don't want to squash yourself into your dad's old banger on a wing and a prayer. Hiring a beautiful, vintage car may add the touch of elegance you deserve. White Rolls-Royces, Cadillacs and Bentleys are all popular wedding choices. If you are happy to use a friend or relative's car, work out who is going to drive it, how many of you can fit inside and how to decorate it, well in advance. And make sure basic things like flat tyres and running out of petrol are planned for.

Horse-drawn carriages, helicopters, speedboats and motorcycle sidecars are now all popular methods of arriving at the service. They are also, however, expensive alternatives, but if you are determined, go for it, just make sure you and your huge meringue can fit in there before you pay the deposit. Also make sure your hairstyle and veil can withstand the elements if you are keen to travel in an open-top, faster-than-the-speed-of-light vehicle.

Ask your chosen vehicle to arrive half an hour before the

set-off time, check that it carries umbrellas in case of a sudden downpour and make sure you are the only bride to be ferried around on that day. You don't want to be late for your ceremony because another couple has overrun.

A second vehicle – to transport the bride's mother and attendants – may seem like unnecessary expenditure. Try asking your chauffeur if he minds doing two trips. This means the bridesmaids and bride's mother will arrive at least twenty minutes before the service, but it will save cash – and they'll be able to greet everyone at the venue and tell them how you are doing (without mentioning your secret dress).

To save even more money, if you live close to the venue, walk instead of hiring a car – it will make a friendly and original impression. If you live quite a distance away, ask someone with a nice car to take you and the bridesmaids. Decorate the car with pretty white or gold ribbons and you're away. Literally.

Pick-a-cake, pick-a-cake

Flavour

Traditionally, a wedding cake is a heavily iced fruitcake of more than one tier, so an individual tier can be saved and stored for the Christening of the couple's first-born. But if you hate fruitcake and icing – and don't know whether you want children or a Christening anyway – steer away from the obvious for some more tasty options.

Some couples serve fortune cookies or fairy cakes as a fun, kitsch option. Others go for profiterole mountains or chocolate-dipped strawberry mounds. If you still want to 'cut the cake' for good luck's sake, try orange, lemon, carrot or coffee. Ginger, rum and raisin, and vanilla are other more unusual choices. Don't worry too much about other people's preferences and go for the flavour and design you want. Most people leave the cake anyway as they've just had the wedding breakfast.

Design

Traditional cakes are often decorated with good-luck symbols: horseshoes and silver bells to ward off evil spirits, flowers to represent innocence and fidelity, and a little bride and groom sitting on the top tier, representing unity.

If you want to get away from the usual three-tier cake, design a cake that means something to you. Any good bakery or confectioner will have books on cake designs and ideas. Perhaps try a cake in the shape of a suitcase to symbolise your new life and your honeymoon, or a magic castle to represent your fairytale romance. If you are from two different countries, you could have a cake iced with the flags of your two nations. Look at wedding and cookery magazines for inspiration.

Let the music play

Picking a first dance that won't make anyone puke or laugh

There is a fine line to tread between romance and slush. You want to walk on the romantic side. Choose a song that means something to both of you – as a couple – but steer clear of the vomit-inducing ballads of Celine Dion and Neil Diamond (unless in exceptional circumstances). Originality counts for a lot – I've been to more than a handful of weddings where the couple dance to *Wonderful Tonight* by Eric Clapton like they were the only ones in the world. Couples usually fall back on the old standards (some even go so low as *The Lady in Red;* are they being sarcastic?) when they haven't given the first dance much thought. This is a big mistake because all your guests will rush to video/photograph/coo at you as soon as you take your initial steps on the dance-floor.

Foolproof plan for first dances

◆ Make sure the music isn't too fast. Too speedy and you'll look like animals on heat.

◆ Check the lyrics. You may like the tune and the chorus may be quite merry, just check the singer doesn't sink into a suicidal depression by the final verse.

◆ Practise. Dance around the kitchen to refine your moves. If you haven't got any moves, pay for dance lessons and learn some. It sounds a bit OTT for one quick twirl around a room, but it's better than treading on each other's toes.

- It is your first dance. Make sure it is played before everyone else hits the dance-floor, but when you're ready. I've been to a wedding where the bride had to dance with the best man because the groom was in the toilet.

- Make sure that the DJ or chosen music maestro has the correct version of the song and it is good quality i.e. a wedding favourite *I've Got You Under My Skin* has been recorded by over ten different artists at different speeds.

Should you musically entertain your guests before the party gets going?

There is a lot of hanging about at weddings. Even if you do without excessive photography and the line-up, there will still be expanses of time when people are standing around with little to do but make small talk. Think about having a musical accompaniment of some sort during drinks and dinner – even if it's just a suitable CD played in the background. More extravagant options are harpists, string quartets or singing impersonators. We had a Dean Martina-like singer during our wedding breakfast, who got everyone dancing on the tables before the speeches and guaranteed a good night ahead.

DJ or live band: which fills the dance-floor quicker?

There is nothing more depressing than a half-empty dance-floor at a wedding reception. You want to look around on your big day and see friends and family getting down and shaking it all around. Not only will this keep your guests away from your frugal buffet but it will make them have the night of their lives. How many people dance depends on how good the music is… so which should you go with?

Pro DJ: can play favourites and requests at a whim, has a good selection of flashing lights and possibly a mirror ball, and will read the mood of the crowd.

Con DJ: has tendency to wear vile clothes and flirt with all the ladies, can give guests attitude when requesting their favourite tunes, can get microphone-hungry and talk through favourite tracks.

Pro live band: draws an instant crowd, and adds a personal, original touch. Nothing beats live music.

Con live band: can normally only play one genre of music, can't play for as long as a DJ and will need to take long breaks, can play up – and strip – for the crowd.

Is karaoke at wedding receptions ever a good idea?

Lots of fun and cheap entertainment – but if you hate it, you *really* hate it, and karaoke always seems to dominate any party. You always get the odd one who hogs the microphone while the others try to hide at the back of the room. Perhaps keep the karaoke for a welcome-home party after the honeymoon.

Wedding list

Is it rude to ask guests for presents?

Everyone – with the exception of the dishearteningly mean – will want to get you a wedding present and your guests will want to get you something you like. This is where a wedding list comes in. It's a perfect solution, both for the couple (who don't wish to receive five toasters and a paint-ing of a horse) and for the guests (who haven't got the time to search around for the perfect gift). Modern wedding lists are the most convenient things. You simply spend a won-derful day dream shopping in your favourite department store, getting excited over implements that you didn't even know existed (lettuce dryers, plastic ice cubes etc.) and then wait for them all to be delivered to your home. Your guests have the easy options of either pretending to go shopping for the gift and then choosing something from your list, or just ringing up the store and buying a perfect gift within their price range without leaving their house.

How do you tell your guests about your wedding list?

It may seem pretty cheeky to include details of the wedding list in with the invitation. It may come across as a threat: 'If I've got to feed you, you'd better buy me something good.' But practicality will win out and most guests will be relieved for the list to fall on to their mat as they open the envelope. It negates the need to ring the couple or the par-ents and enquire if they have a list and if so where is it held. Most stores now supply elegant, neat wedding list cards to enclose with the invites.

How do you cope with freestylers?

Some guests will approach you before the day and say they'd like to get you something personal – not from the official list – would this be okay? Of course, your answer is yes. Even if you suspect this is because they want to give you something cheap from the market, or that they finally want to off-load that old toaster that is gathering dust in their loft, be gracious. For every cheapo who gives you a personal salt and pepper set which they think 'is more you than the one you picked on the list', you will have someone that has seen an amazing painting, book or gift vouchers which are perfect and that you hadn't thought of.

> **NB In the event of five toasters – don't panic**. Count your-self lucky you have one good toaster and return the others to the department store. When each toaster-donator visits your home, pretend that is their one. If there are no receipts and you can't return the goods, charity shops and students are always willing to take things off your hands. A wedding list should keep this to a minimum.

What things should you put on your wedding list?

As a rule, your wedding list should set you up for the whole of your married life. Even if you are not drinking cham-pagne from fine crystal now, if you hope to be in ten years time, put the glasses down on your list. Visit the store up to six months before the wedding – they can only manage a limited number of lists and they get booked up quickly – and visit every department, even if you are bored by the prospect of spending the afternoon in the gardening section. As well as being sensible though, list some fun, personal gifts that aren't long-term investments but short-term fancies. We put down a multi-coloured water tower that bubbles in time with music. We thought people would ignore it, but the more imaginative guests fought over who would buy it first. A good idea is to go through every room in an imaginary house – even if you're still living in a shoe-box bedsit – and work out what you need for each room. Think about kitchen appliances and gadgets, crockery and cutlery, furniture, electrical appliances, table linen, bedding, towels, tools and garden equipment.

When should the gifts be delivered?

Some people like taking the gifts to the wedding and handing them personally to the bride and groom. This is a nice idea but things can go missing and presents confused. We had a phantom power drill with no gift tag on it at our wedding, which we felt terrible about because we didn't know who to thank. If you get gifts on the day, have someone in charge of putting them somewhere safe. In many ways, it's nice to have the gifts delivered to your home a few weeks after the honeymoon. Although you have picked the items out, it's like Christmas – and after the wedding and honeymoon it's good to have something to look forward to.

Secrets of Success

♦ Remember to send maps, directions and hotel information with invitations. It will save you lots of time and hassle in the long run.

♦ If the wedding is at noon, the invitation should say noon, not 12 o'clock or 12.00 noon.

♦ Minimise scribbling and waste paper when arranging the table plan by writing everyone's name on an individual piece of paper. Divide the names into different groups until you have found the perfect combination – and only then write out the final table plan.

♦ Ask friends to design the table plan and name-places for you. Lure your girlfriends over to your place with a bottle of wine and ask them to help write the invitations. If you know any computer whiz kids, perhaps they can even design the invitations for you. Remember: wedding invitations don't have to be sent first class. Save money by sending them second class or delivering them by hand.

◆ If you can't face the table plan, let everyone sort themselves out. Place two bowls full of numbers in the reception room, one for the boys and one for the girls. Ask guests to pick a number from the bowl as they arrive. This will mix people up fairly and without you getting a headache. However, some people may find the idea abhorrent, because weddings are the only chances they get to speak to certain people.

◆ Prior to the formal invitations being sent out, you could think about sending personal letters to close friends and family to let them know you've set the date. This will make sure everyone you want to be there will be there. The more notice people get, the easier it will be for them to change holiday dates etc.

◆ To keep flowers fresh and perky, spray them liberally with cool water and store them in a cool, dark place.

◆ Although fresh flowers are the favourite because of their smell and freshness, hyperallergic guests will be grateful for a pollen-free environment, so don't sneer at silk or parchment fakes straight away. They are more costly, but last longer and are sneeze-free. If you do go for fresh flowers, think about mixing them with fresh herbs, which were traditionally used at weddings to ward off bad spirits and to bring good luck.

◆ Find the time to check the flowers before the service. As much as you trust your mother, mother-in-law or partner, you don't want to leave it all up to them and be disappointed when you arrive at the venue.

◆ In the summer months, cut down on flowers with a high pollen count. You don't want your hay fever-suffering guests sneezing and spluttering through the sentimental parts of the ceremony.

◆ Don't let the florist go too mad with huge arrangements in doorways and at the end of the pews. Too flamboyant and you could be shuffling and ducking along the aisle like a paranoid FBI agent.

◆ Decorate your tables with tea lights inside glasses. Buy special glass paint from an art supplier and inscribe the wedding date and your names on them. Your guests can take them home as a memento. Another way to dress the tables is to put hand-picked flowers into a clean jam jar or tin. This looks rustic and pretty, especially when tied with ribbon, and is much cheaper than a formal centrepiece. Sprinkle glitter on the table for an extra twinkle.

◆ You can save – and make a fortune – by using lottery tickets in pretty envelopes as a wedding favour and place-name in one. It will be an exciting gift to greet the guests, and you could make a fortune by collecting forgotten tickets at the end of the evening.

◆ Buy your wedding ring from the same place your partner bought the engagement ring and the jeweller will probably do any adjustments for free.

◆ If you don't want a gold, white gold or platinum wedding band, don't choose that metal for your engagement ring.

◆ If money is tight, don't commission a wedding cake, buy one from a supermarket or bakery. If you want a special design, bake the cake yourself and then get a professional to ice it. A further saver is to serve the cake as the dessert with coffee.

- If you decide to have music during the reception, beware of placing people too near the speakers. Allow a 2.5 metre (8 foot) radius around each speaker or your guests might be deaf and hoarse by the end of the night.

- For a more personal and thrifty approach, instead of hiring a DJ, make a compilation tape or CD of your favourite songs. If you think they're fantastic, your friends probably will too and the dance-floor will be packed all night.

- Wedding lists are political and no one wants to be the first to break into a set of cutlery, glass or china. If you really want them, ask a good friend to get something from the set specifically to get the ball rolling.

- Releasing details of a wedding list for a second marriage may seem a little mercenary, particularly when many of the guests have already forked out once. Leave the choice of gifts up to the guests, but popular choices are flowers, plants and gift vouchers.

- When choosing sets of china or glasses for your wedding list, put an extra two of everything to allow for breakages during married life – and no, I don't mean during arguments.

- Don't allow only a few hours to complete your wedding list – you'll need a whole day, if not more, by the time you've filled in all your details and toured the whole store.

- On your wedding list, remember to include items from all price ranges – and always push the price levels higher than you'd expect. Families and friends often like to club together to buy a substantial gift. Ring the wedding bureau at the store on a regular basis to see how the list is going and if you need to go back in to add some more items.

- Use the Ideal time planner to chart your progress.

Chapter Four

Service with a smile

N THE EXCITEMENT over the cosmetic details of a wedding, the most important aspect of the day – both spiritually and legally – is often forgotten. While brides-to-be spend weeks agonising over fruit or sponge, silk or satin, they barely spend a few minutes deciding who will marry them to their partner and how. This is a shame. Not only because this is the part of the day when you actually get to tell the world how in love you are with your partner, but also because today there are so many fun, exotic and flamboyant options open to every couple. It really is a buyer's market. You can get the service you've always dreamed of – even if you've fantasised about getting married on a camel in a desert with the Spice Girls playing as you say your vows. You may be admitted to some form of asylum when you return from honeymoon, but if that's the ceremony you want, it's all yours.

Church or civil?

When deciding on the service that you want, choosing between a religious and civil ceremony is the biggest dilemma. If your parents follow a particular religion and you were raised as such, they will normally be disappointed if you go for a civil ceremony. If you want a religious ceremony but have not attended church for as long as you can remember, your friends may think you are being hypocritical. Follow your heart. Only you and your partner can decide if saying religious vows in a place of worship will mean more to you than any other place.

Church weddings

For a church wedding, the first thing to do is contact your favoured minister to get his consent. Most ministers are pretty welcoming to young couples who would like to have a religious ceremony. It really all depends on the minister's personal rules on divorcees, cohabiters, non-virgins, non-churchgoers and people who live outside their favoured parish. Don't give up if one vicar says no because you are 'living in sin' for example, another more liberal minister may welcome you with open arms. As long as you are baptised, there are no official problems. If you have no luck at all but still want to add a religious aspect to your day, ask a minister if they will perform a service of blessing for you and your partner.

When trying to find a religious venue, ask as soon as possible because churches – particularly historic or pretty ones – get booked up years in advance. And remember, once s/he has accepted you, s/he may ask you to attend church regularly until the wedding. The church may also insist you attend their marriage-guidance classes. Before you can have a church service, the banns will need to be read. The banns is a legal notice that allows people to register their objections to your proposed marriage. Many people think this is more complicated than it is, and the church is looking towards updating its system soon. Don't panic, once the minister has read your banns, the only objections that are seriously considered are if you are already married or trying to marry a family relation.

The vows
Around the time your banns are read, speak to the vicar about your favoured wording for the service. You do not have to promise to 'obey' unless you want to. You can say 'cherish' or another similar word, so ask your minister. The vows at a church wedding are not open for interpretation, so to personalise your service you can add favourite passages from the bible or poems and readings before and after the vows are exchanged. One advantage of having a civil ceremony is that you can write your own vows and service. If you want to promise to 'call him Snooklebum forever', then go ahead – if you can face the laughter.

Top five biblical readings
First Epistle of St John, Chapter 4, Verses 7–12
Epistle to the Ephesians, Chapter 3, Verse 14 to end
Ecclesiastes, Chapter 3, Verses 1–8

Gospel of St John, Chapter 14, Verses 9–12
First Epistle to the Corinthians, Chapter 13

Top five church tunes
'Wedding March' from *A Midsummer Night's Dream* by Mendelssohn
'Wedding March' from *The Marriage of Figaro* by Mozart
The Arrival of the Queen of Sheba by Handel
'Grand March' from *Aida* by Verdi
'Ave Maria' by Schubert

Top five hymns
'Lord of the Dance'
'Love Divine all Loves Excelling'
'Praise my Soul, the King of Heaven'
'All Things Bright and Beautiful'
'Make Me a Channel of Your Peace'

Other religions

Every religious ceremony is completely different – there could be a book written about each one on its own. The general rule across all faiths is to speak to the officiating minister at your chosen place of worship as soon as possible. He or she will act as your guide and take you through the legal framework of getting married. In many cases, you may need to have a registry office wedding before the religious service to make your marriage legally binding. In other instances, a registrar may be welcome to attend the religious service and complete all the required documents at the same time.

Can mixed faith couples have a religious service?

Different faiths have different views on marrying someone who is a different religion, and although you personally may not have objections to your partner's faith, your parents or other family members might. A good level of communication and understanding is required for inter-faith marriages to work. But statistics prove that they can – and normally do – develop into long-term, healthy partnerships. Within religious groups, there are different levels of tolerance. Orthodox Jews and Muslims will expect a person with a non-similar faith to convert, while most other religions are more lenient. Many couples decide to hold two separate ceremonies to keep both families happy, or even rebel and have a civil ceremony – but incorporating elements of both faiths into the service.

SEEMA, 26

❝ Being a Hindu I had always envisaged having a religious ceremony spoken in the Indian language and wearing the traditional red sari. However, I had not bargained on marrying a white, atheist lad from South Wales. It could have been difficult, but we decided to combine the two cultures. My fiancé rose to the occasion by wearing a customary Nehru jacket, making vows in Indian that he did not understand and shaking his bootie to Asian tunes. Many of the English guests were surprised to see a raging fire form part of the ceremony and, probably, disappointed at the distinct lack of alcohol present. Of course, all the rules changed for the British wedding the following week. It was a civil ceremony in a hotel on a cliff-top somewhere deep in South Wales. This time however, in an attempt to counter the seriousness of the Hindu ceremony we made the day a little more light-hearted. ❞

How easy is it for a couple from two different countries to get married?

Difficulties vary from country to country. For either a civil or religious ceremony, the person in the couple getting married outside of their country will need to provide copies of their birth certificate, proof of residency and a certificate of no impediment to marriage. The best thing to do is to check with the foreign consul or embassy of both countries involved. This will also ensure that the marriage will be considered legal and binding in his or her own country.

Is it difficult to organise a wedding in another country?

Getting married on the white, sandy beaches of Cyprus or under the dazzling lights of Las Vegas is a growing trend. Combining a wedding with a honeymoon is cost and time efficient – and it also means you can limit the guest list to your nearest and dearest. The greatest benefit is that because you are miles away from the chosen location, someone does all the planning for you. You pick the venue and the menu, and then a wedding planner will fill in the gaps – you can spend all your time choosing a suitable dress for a sunset wedding next to the ocean. Travel agents are offering a vast amount of packages and they will advise you on what documents you need before you go out to your wedding destination. Sometimes you have to be in a country for a minimum time before they allow a ceremony to take place, but just look at this as extra de-stressing and sunbathing time. The initial costs may seem extortionate – only the best hotels offer wedding packages and the prices reflect this – but remember that once it's paid, it's paid. And all the money is going on you both and your honeymoon, rather than on a crowd of rowdy relatives, who you haven't seen for five years, to get drunk.

NB If you decide to get married abroad, you may feel sad that many people will not be able to celebrate with you. Budget for a party when you get home for friends and distant relatives and maybe have a first dance and cut the wedding cake there, so they can take some pictures and feel like they are part of your wedding.

Civil ceremonies

Although civil ceremonies often seem like the sensible option – either because of faith, finances, time or interests – couples often panic that this is the lesser option, almost that a wedding held outside of a religious building doesn't mean as much. What civil ceremonies really offer is freedom. The venues and vows may not be as austere, traditional and impressive as religious ones, but you can adapt everything about your wedding to suit you. Because of this, it can reflect your personalities better than anything else. The only restraint really is that you cannot have any religious reading during the service. Apart from that, it's all down to you. Have fun.

Where can a civil ceremony be held?

Practically anywhere. Ask your local council for a list of authorised venues as they are expanding all the time. Today, you can probably get married anywhere from the pitch of your favourite football team to your old university dining room. As long as an official registrar attends to sanction the marriage legally, the world is your oyster – or a potential venue at least. Think carefully before you decide – many venues are cottoning on to their popularity and charging outlandish prices for a few tables in a field. In other cases, what might seem like a wacky idea before your wedding, in reality might be a little too informal and disorganised.

How can we put our personal stamp on a civil ceremony?

Getting married in a registry office or hotel conference room can often be rather bland and uniform, so spice it up with a few inspired choices. Play your favourite song as you walk up the aisle – you won't have any constraints and can dance up to the latest Madonna record if you wish. You are not allowed religious readings, so ask your friends and family to write and/or read poems for you, or to read your favourite childhood nursery rhyme, or even to tell a few (appropriate) wedding jokes. In a civil ceremony, you can add anything you like to the vows (you can even promise to wash and darn his socks forever more, if you so desire), and the official will say, 'You may now kiss the bride' at the end of the ceremony. The congregation will also feel more inclined to laugh, cheer and clap during a civil ceremony than at a more old-fashioned religious one.

HOLLIE, 26

❝ Steve and I were married on a beautiful sunny day in June. My favourite memory of the day was the moment when I turned to walk down the aisle and saw Steve, with his eyes full of tears, wearing the biggest smile I have ever seen. We had a civil ceremony at an approved venue: an old Jacobean hall set in beautiful grounds in the countryside of Hertfordshire. I was a little sceptical when we decided to have a civil ceremony – and I *know* my mum was convinced that it would be unromantic and brief – but the registrar who conducted our service made it wonderful. He talked about the history and importance of marriage and involved our guests by making them stand for the legal parts of the ceremony. All in all, it lasted 40 minutes and everyone commented afterwards on how special it had been. ❞

How to make a grand entrance?

There are so many things to think about in those three minutes you've got to pull yourself together before your date with destiny. Don't trip over; don't laugh; don't cry; try to control the blushing; try not to faint; don't fart. All these fears, and yet you are determined to look the most elegant and serene you have ever looked in your life. Who needs this stress? First thing to remember is that everyone is there for you, they are good friends and family and they care about you – otherwise they wouldn't be there. Second thing to remember is that they are all wishing you well and are excited about seeing your dress. Third thing to remember is your posture. Stand straight – but not like you've got a metal pole stuck where the sun don't shine – and take small, deliberate steps towards the front. I ran so fast up the aisle that I came out as a streak of lightening in pictures and people still comment on what a shame it was even now. Brief the person who is giving you away: they are there to support you, but emotionally rather than physically. You don't want their arms all over you, pulling you along or holding you back. Make sure your entrance music is at the right volume. Too quiet and no one will know you've arrived. Too loud and you'll feel like Suzi Quatro arriving for a gig at Glastonbury, and not a blushing bride.

Secrets of Success

◆ It may seem like a fun idea to have a double wedding with a best friend or a favoured sibling but you are asking for trouble. It's hard enough getting what you want when there are just two of you, let alone four. And the service could run the risk of being as tacky as a Jerry Springer-esque televised ceremony.

◆ Whatever ceremony you want, if you are having readings, choose people who can withstand the pressure of standing in front of lots of strangers and playing a major part in your wedding. In a way, their task is even worse than that of the speechmakers at the reception – they won't have had a chance (hopefully) to get to the bar yet.

◆ If you are planning to get married abroad, check that the service will be performed in your language. It would be a shame to miss your entire wedding because your schoolgirl French is a little poor.

◆ If you are having a church wedding and want bellringers and a choir, check they have such things. They don't come as standard and a lack of these elements may affect a couple's final choice. If you are having a civil ceremony and wish to play a favoured piece of music as you walk in, pick someone reliable to press play on the stereo system. There's nothing worse than walking in to silence .

◆ Check with the venue that they will allow photography and video recording. Many religious institutions restrict photography during prayers and the exchanging of vows, but each place is different, so ask.

◆ There is usually a rehearsal a week or so before the wedding so that all parties know what they are doing and when they should be doing it. If you are having a civil ceremony and this is not an option, visit the venue with the key players to get them used to the size of the room and the exits and entrances. It will minimise mishaps on the day.

◆ It is advisable to pay service fees in advance – you'll have enough things to think about on the day.

◆ If you are marrying in church, ask the vicar if another couple are getting married the same day. If so, consult each other on colours and styles of flowers and you've halved your florist's bill.

◆ Although it is traditional for the father of the bride to walk his daughter down the aisle at her wedding – whether you are having a religious or civil ceremony – this is just a tradition and can be adapted. Both parents can accompany you on your final walk as a single woman, or your mother alone. You can also walk on your own, with your bridesmaids, or with your own children, if you have any.

◆ Churchyards are particularly mucky and get muddy quickly in bad weather. To arrive in pristine condition, lay plastic sheeting or if the worst comes to the worst, hoist up your dress and wear plastic carrier bags on each foot.

◆ At an autumn or winter wedding, nothing inspires romance and intimacy like a candlelit wedding service. Just don't place the candles too near the floral displays or your dress, or near where guests can accidentally brush against them. Candles should never be left burning unattended.

◆ Keep service sheets from every other wedding you attend in the run-up to you own. This is a good way of getting music and reading suggestions – and may even help you with printing and colour-scheme ideas.

Chapter Five

Looking like a princess without having to behave like one

WHEN YOU ARE DRESSED up to the nines and everyone is telling you how amazing you look, it's easy to stop being you and start being a self-obsessed cow. Try not to let all the glamour, attention and excitement go to your head. Even on wedding days, beauty comes from within.

The beauty myth

On holiday in Cyprus, I remarked on what a beautiful setting it would make for a dream wedding. The hotel manager replied, 'Yes, it's a beautiful setting, it's just a shame that so many ugly brides get in the way and spoil the view.' Okay, this man was a vicious queen with misogynistic tendencies, but he made his point. It is not enough to rely on the virginal radiance of a bride, you have to work at it ladies. And if that means hours of waxing, plucking, dying, cutting, exercising and eating sensibly, so be it. You will not be an ugly blot on the landscape. This is your day and you are going to look like a princess.

Define your personal style

The most important thing to remember when choosing your dress, accessories and hairstyle for the day is that you can't please everyone. Someone is going to think you look over the top, and someone else is going to think you haven't made an effort. So, with your partner's opinions in mind on what makes you look good, go out and pick your dream dress and your fantasy shoes, and spend a fortune getting your hair cut just the way you've always wanted it to be. You're the one that is going to have to be dressed up in it all and your partner is the one who is going to have to look at you for the rest of his life, so you two are the only ones that matter.

Choosing that dream dress

Why do brides have to dress up as overcautious beekeepers (protective net veil and insect-attracting bouquet) on their wedding day while men can get away with a smart suit that they can wear again and again? Depending on your point of view, brides either have it good (you enjoy the glitz and glamour of the occasion) or bad (you're a jeans and trainers girl and the thought of wearing a huge dress and veil makes you feel silly).

History of the wedding dress

Well, sorry girls, but brides have always been made to dress up more than the men on their wedding days. In ancient Rome, the bridal colour was bright yellow and the women were decorated with as many jewels as her family could muster up from the village. In Chinese societies throughout history, the woman has been wrapped in elaborate red, green and gold fabrics, to symbolise wealth, health and happiness. In pre-Victorian Britain, women wore any good fabrics that their families could get their hands on, regardless of colour, except for the royal brides who were always decked out in silver. We have Queen Victoria to thank for our current trend. She opted for a white gown when she married Prince Albert in 1840.

Today, other colours are coming through, but white and ivory remain the most popular. Many brides toy with the idea of red, lavender, green and purple, only to fall back on the traditional dress when it comes to finally choosing. Picking a dress that varies from the norm is very brave and admirable if it is what you have always wanted to do. Just make sure you are happy and secure enough in your choice to cope with the funny looks and nasty asides that may occur. When it comes to weddings, the guests want to see their bride in a long white gown, veil and beautiful bouquet. This might be what you want too, if it's not, sod them. Shock them in a fluorescent-pink dress and matching slingbacks. Remember though, if you are superstitious, green is seen as the kiss of death for a happy marriage.

Finding the right style for you

You have to be sensible and stick to a style that will flatter your figure and suit your wedding service and the time of year you are getting hitched. If you don't you could feel uncomfortable all day and end up sulking in a taffeta heap behind the DJ's booth.

Tall: if you are happy with your height, go for heels and a sweeping gown in one shade. If not, nothing is worse than a bride with bad posture, so choose a two-piece in contrasting colours to break up the expanse of fabric and remove height.

Petite: heels are the obvious option, but be careful not to go mad in stilettos and risk breaking your neck. The simpler the design of the dress, the taller it will make you appear; add a train for an extra few inches.

Curvy: play up your womanly figure with a fishtail gown. Sexy and sophisticated, this dress clings to all the right places – and exaggerates a neat waist. The hourglass shape suits most bridal gowns, so play it up – modern fashions of jeans and T-shirts don't appreciate this shape enough.

Athletic: add definition to a slim frame by adding details. Cowl necks flatter the flat-chested and an empire-line cut will nip in the waist. Muscly arms can be disguised with an organza wrap or a shawl.

Bottom-heavy: match an elaborate slimline top with a simple full skirt for the perfect Cinderella shape that hides all sins. A pointed corset will give the impression of proportioned hips and legs, and abundant netting will disguise whether the curves are your own or a fashion statement. Avoid lycra.

Top-heavy: the boning in a corset will add definition for a perfect shape. A corset should fit like a glove and will eliminate the need to wear a bra for even the larger cup-sizes. If you don't fancy that, choose something with a v-neck to flatter a generous cleavage. Avoid high collars and roll necks at all costs.

Re-evaluating your dream dress

Do you have a fantasy dress? As a child did you rip out pictures of fairy brides from books and magazines and stuff them in your secret drawer? As an adult, did you riffle through *Hello!* and *OK!* tearing out photographs of Catherine Zeta-Douglas and Victoria Beckham and file them carefully in your 'when I'm a bride' hope chest?

If so, now might be the time to re-evaluate your choices. The style might not suit your shape, fashions will have changed, and replicating a $25,000 Versace gown from nothing might not be practical. Assign your cuttings to part of your history and splash out on recent wedding magazines to get some fresh, realistic ideas. If you are determined to have your dream dress, whatever the difficulty or the cost, then just go for it. Why waste time trailing around the shops and flicking through countless pages of dress advertisements when you have your dream dress – albeit on a piece of paper – in front of you. Spend your time locating a brilliant dress designer or seamstress instead.

Who to take shopping and where to go

Try to remember, dress shopping should be fun. It's the one part of the planning that is purely for you. This should be your chance to fulfil all your fantasies. Only take people with you who are going to be encouraging and make an event of it. Perhaps arrange to go out with your mum and bridesmaids afterwards for lunch to celebrate. The pressure is on to look the best you've ever looked, so it can be stressful – help yourself out by avoiding shops with rude assistants and small changing rooms. To try on a wedding dress, you need a big space. Cramming into a normal-sized cubicle will not make the best impression.

Ready-to-wear, made-to-measure or hired?

With the enormous number of bridal shops and designers around, the wide choice of gown means you can really choose what kind of dress you want. There are pros and cons to all the places you can get your dress, it really depends on your plans for the day.

Ready-to-wear

This is probably the quickest and easiest option for a bride with little time to sort out her dress. She can literally go into any of the shops dotted around every town in the country, find her dream dress, try it on off-the-peg and – *voilà* – pay for it and it's all hers. No fussing around with fittings, meetings with the designer, paying deposits and final adjustments. Ready-to-wear is often cheaper than made-to-measure too, as they are designed and produced in bulk. Buying ready-to-wear also means if you are brave enough you can take your dress with you while you go shopping for accessories. This means you can get the colour and style exactly right and you'll have no nasty shocks on the big day.

The downside to ready-to-wear is that you cannot get a perfect fit. The female shape on which these dresses are based doesn't really exist (or very rarely). If your waist and hips fit snugly you can be sure that it will be a little tight under the arms or around the chest. You either have to put up with this – valuing the savings and convenience – or take it to another dressmaker to get it sorted out. And that kind of contradicts the reason you bought ready-to-wear in the first place. Buying a dress off-the-peg will not allow for any weight fluctuations before the wedding day either.

Made-to-measure

This is the ideal and the most popular choice. On average 60 per cent of brides now have their dresses made especially for them. It's a nice feeling to know that something has been made just for you – for most women it will be the only unique item of clothing they will ever own. If you can't spoil yourself on your wedding day when can you? Finding a made-to-measure style that suits you is the best chance you have of looking a million dollars on the day. It can be modified, enhanced and shaped to be everything you dreamed of.

Early enquiries are essential. Designers ask for between three to six months' notice to make a dress, so this is not often possible if you are having a quickie wedding. Make sure you have a good relationship with the designer. She could be the greatest wedding dressmaker in the world, but if she won't go along with your wishes and price frame she is of no use to you at all. Help yourself by taking a sketch or photograph of your dream dress along with you to the first few meetings. If you are unsure of what you want, visit a few dress shops to see what style suits you before it starts being made. The thing about made-to-measure is you can't change your mind. Or if you do, it is going to cost you a fortune.

JULIE, 32

❝ Dress shopping was the part I'd been really looking forward to, but I was disappointed by many shops: I got a few sullen teenagers who didn't know the first thing about sizes or styles, and the display dresses were grubby and only available in sample sizes. I was feeling really disheartened when I came across a small, family-run boutique in London. You'd have thought they were making their own daughter's dress, they put so much effort into it. I had many fittings until it was perfect. So look around, don't settle for anything less than supportive staff and good-quality gowns. ❞

Hired

This is by far the cheapest option. Hiring could be the only way you can realistically afford to wear your dream designer dress. Prices to hire are between 25–50 per cent of full retail price. The hire shops keep prices down by lending gowns out on an average of four times to various brides. Don't worry about the condition of the dress; all gowns are dry-cleaned and maintained thoroughly so a hired gown will look and feel as good as new, as long as you go to a reputable boutique.

Hiring could be a good thing but many brides won't like the fact that hired dresses are simple and made of easily cleaned fabrics. Beadwork and embroidery tends not to dry-clean very well so you might not find a wide variety of designs. The other factor against hired dresses is that you can't keep them. It is true, that after the wedding it will probably be shut up in a suitcase or thrown into the loft, but it is kind of nice knowing you have it all the same. It will probably never happen, but if she wanted to, your daughter could wear it when she is a bride. The other good thing about buying your dress is that you can do what you want in it and not worry about it getting ruined. I've seen brides rolling about on the floor and downing funnels of Black Russian (not the most elegant of weddings), and even I got so excited Riverdancing that my straps fell off. Even if you are quite contained, you can't account for other people stepping on your dress, the weather or spillages. If you are in a hired dress, your anxiety could ruin the day.

A modern girl's other options

Many brides are rebelling from the big, white dress thing and looking for something sleeker and more cutting edge. If you fit into this category, visit the evening wear sections of big department stores. They will offer a range of stylish and suitable cocktail or evening dresses that can easily replace a larger gown. This is a good idea if you are holding your wedding abroad. Handling a long train is difficult enough in a church, let alone on a beach on a windy, hot day. This will give you a great opportunity to really splash out on a dream dress that you will be able to wear again and again, at parties, balls and dinner dances. Many brides insist they will be able to customise their gowns for such occasions but I've never met a bride who has actually got round to it yet! Another option is a classic two-piece suit in white, cream or beige – effortlessly elegant, understated and timeless. Play it up with beautiful accessories and you have a totally modern and relaxed outfit for your wedding. Your dad might not like it – it may seem a little too radical – but you'll feel like the coolest kid on the block (which is how you should feel on your wedding day).

Over-accessorising – the eighth deadly sin

A friend of mine once went to the wedding of a purple fanatic. The bride was covered head-to-toe in her favourite colour. She wore an elaborate purple gown, fastened with maroon buttons and decorated with mauve bows. Through the holes in her violet sandals, her toes peeped out, each digit an ever increasing hue. Being quite a large girl, the colour did nothing to hide the areas that should be hidden. Even her hair was purple, which led to hysterical chanting during the groom's favourite hymn 'All Things Bright and Beautiful': 'that purple-headed mountain'. To add to the hair, the dress, the shoes and the nail polish was a full face of slap (all different shades of purple), a BA Baracus from the A-team amount of jewellery (all different shades of purple), and instead of a bouquet she held a lace and sequin parasol (which was also in different shades of purple).

How do you balance over-exuberance with good taste?

It's easily done. On your wedding day, when you learn to focus on every small detail and decoration from table settings to personalised matchboxes, when it comes to dressing yourself, it is easy to focus on the small things rather than the big picture. You may have seen three beautiful necklaces, but you only need one. Anything more will over-egg the pudding. If you have chosen delicate slippers, don't match them with jewel-encrusted stockings and a fussy suspender belt, you'll ruin the look altogether. If your dream dress has lots of detail on the sleeves, you don't want to go covering them up, however much you like the stole or pashmina you've spotted in your favourite shop.

More than ever, on your wedding day remember: less is more.

To diet or not to diet?

The pressure is on. You've just announced you are getting married in twelve months' time. Your female friends and family members congratulate you, ooh and aah a little and gossip with you about your choice of flowers. And then they come out with what they really want to know, or rather, they come out with sugar-coated advice: 'I suppose you'll be going on a diet then, dear, won't you?' They raise their eyebrows expectantly. They pray that you will see sense and realise before the big day that your arse really is too big to be the centre of attention as you walk down the aisle to meet your destiny.

HAYLEY, 29

❝ Instead of congratulating me on my engagement my mother said, 'Well this is the perfect time to do something about your weight now isn't it.' She even went so far as slapping my thighs and bottom and tutting, 'You'll have to get rid of these if you've got any chance of being a beautiful bride.' I was devastated. I starved myself until the wedding, becoming a miserable cow in the process, then as soon as I got back from my honeymoon I started stocking up on all the food I'd missed. I've now ballooned two dress sizes past my original, stable weight. I suppose I did look better in the photos – but I felt a little faint. ❞

A weighty paranoia sets in

You always thought your bottom was all right. I mean, not great, but along with your other bits – your legs, your upper arms, your tummy – it kind of suited you, and more importantly, it is your natural body shape. You've never overeaten, starved yourself, or followed faddish diets. So why, on the eve of the most stressful event of your life, are your loved ones suggesting you cut down on the calories? If anything, this will just increase the level of tension in the house as the big day beckons. All girls know that the quickest way to stop an argument, nervous breakdown, mood swing is the arrival of a family-size bar of Galaxy Hazelnut chocolate.

Learn to be comfortable in your own skin

I didn't diet at all. People kept hinting that I should, but I kept reminding them of a few things:

◆ My husband fell in love with me the way I am so why would I suddenly change myself now.

◆ I didn't have the time or the inclination to start worrying about my weight. There was enough to do without weighing rice and grains every few hours and feeling guilty if I enjoyed a pizza with friends. A stress-busting swim was my only concession to weight control.

◆ I wasn't fat. I was a size 14, six foot, and healthy. Okay, I didn't fit into most people's ideals of a skinny, feminine girl but I felt comfortable in my own skin and rebelled against the idea of starving myself. This was my basic shape so everyone else just had to deal with it.

Slimming tricks

If you lack the willpower or inclination, here are a few last-minute emergency measures to slim you down for the big day:

◆ Thigh-grip tights are a Godsend. Available from all good department stores and larger chemists, this hosiery sucks and gathers in your flabby bits and can take you down a dress size in an instant. Don't ask where all the fat goes, no one knows, it just disappears. Give a spare pair to your mum or chief bridesmaid to look after in case you ladder them. Not being able to fit back in your dress halfway through the evening would be very embarrassing.

◆ Take your underwear with you when you are having your final dress fitting. This will ensure a neat fit and a lack of lumps. Nothing makes a dress look more ill fitting than a glimpse of bra strap or visible panty line.

♦ Minimiser bras work wonders for the fuller busted. They smooth your chest to give a neater fit across your front and make sure that buttons don't pull. Or as a one-off treat, how about having a bra made especially for you? This will give the perfect lift and shape.

♦ Steer clear of fussy details. Bows, bells and ruching are definite no-nos. Clean lines and good tailoring will give the neatest shape. Bustiers are particularly good at streamlining your boobs and waist, and fuller skirts will cover a multitude of sins.

♦ Have your dress made for you. It will be a little more expensive than buying off-the-peg, but this is the only way you will find a perfect fit, and the dressmaker will be able to use her skills to accentuate and camouflage your best and worst bits.

♦ High heels make legs look longer and therefore slimmer – but practise first if you're not used to walking in them. Tripping down the aisle is not a good look.

The sensible way to lose weight?

Just learn to eat everything in moderation. Perhaps you shouldn't grab a McDonald's after work every night for convenience but a little of what you fancy does do you good. So rather than panicking about your weight and starving yourself, just eat a few more pieces of fruit and vegetables and a little less fat. Ignore faddish diets like the cabbage soup and egg regime. You may lose the weight but you won't smell very nice and you'll loose all your energy.

You need something to soak up the alcohol on your hen night and fainting in church is just so *passé*.

Unfortunately exercise does work

Exercise is the key to any sustainable weight loss so join a gym or encourage your friends to go out running with you. The thought is depressing isn't it? I know, believe me, but as soon as you do it once and the feel-good endorphins start flowing through your system, it won't be so hard to keep it up. It will also help to relieve some of the tension between you, your mother and her over-indulgent guest list.

> **NB Some brides do lose weight unintentionally.** A wedding, however enjoyable ultimately, is stressful and with all your spare time spent running around, chasing things and panicking, a few loose pounds could drop off. Don't rely on this, however, look on it as a bonus. Also, as the day beckons, people will tell you that you are losing weight when you haven't. It's what they assume every modern girl wants to hear in the run-up to the wedding. Accept their remarks graciously, laugh to yourself and then buy a packet of Ferrero Rocher on the way home.

Beauty treats to make you look and feel brilliant

The issue of weight aside, there are many other things a bride-to-be can do to make sure she is at optimum gorgeousness on her wedding day. This means being groomed within an inch of your life. Think Gwyneth Paltrow on a good day. Or even better, think Audrey Hepburn in *Breakfast at Tiffany's*. I'm not suggesting you start hanging out with criminals and male gigolos, but a few hours in a beauty salon wouldn't go amiss.

Look on these beauty fixers as a benefit to your whole being, inside and out, and you won't resent the high prices and long waiting lists. You'll be glowing so much, you won't notice the hole in your wallet.

Waxing

More than anything – don't forget this! You don't want to throw your arms above your head to launch the bouquet at a gathered gaggle of women and be faced with a crop of hair. The French feminist look has never been in for brides. Wax away. Yes it's painful but no other method gives such a clean, smooth finish. And just think, you'll be able to go away on honeymoon knowing you don't have to worry about regrowth for at least a week. Take the plunge and give yourself a Brazilian bikini wax – apparently men go mad for it, so it could be a nice surprise for your husband on your first night of wedded bliss. While you are biting the therapist's chair in agony – ask her to pluck your eyebrows for you. A well-shaped brow flatters every face shape.

Facials

If you decide you want to get your skin sorted out for your wedding, start a course of facials a few months before the day. Skin acts differently to different types of creams, cleansers and exfoliators so you want time to find the perfect package for you. Facials give the face a healthy shine but can encourage outbreaks of blemishes after the first few treatments. This is all good stuff – the impurities are leaving the skin – but you don't want to be spotty on the great day, so that's another reason to start early.

Teeth whitening

All the stars have it done – how else do they keep those Hollywood grins so dazzling. Despite being a one-off treatment, prices are high and people do complain of sensitivity to hot and cold for a few days after. Opt to have whitening done by a dentist to minimise side effects – they get better results and the bleaches they use are less abrasive to the enamel than over-the-counter cleaners.

Cellulite treatments

Unrelated to weight, age or sex, doctors say cellulite is a mixture of bad luck and bad lifestyle. Exercise doesn't shift it but a range of products on the market claim to. Hundreds of beauty editors swear by them, so check out your favourite magazine or department store for the latest wonder products. Also try drinking a minimum of two litres (four pints) of water every day, dry body-brushing problem areas and taking herbal supplements. Juniper berry capsules are great for circulation and natural cleansing. Grapefruit and lemon aid digestion and fluid retention.

Fake tanning

We all know we are not supposed to use sunbeds anymore – they promote ageing, skin cancer and lacerations. A few visits to the solarium won't kill you but a safe option is to try out the numerous self-tanning products on the market. Don't worry, they are not orange like they used to be and the smell has improved dramatically. Just make sure you exfoliate your whole body first, moisturise well then apply sparingly, paying particular attention to the elbows, knees and neck (these are the areas that tend to look grubby).

Don't go mad – a deep tan in the middle of a month of bad weather will look odd, especially when you get the photos back and the rest of the congregation looks pale and wan.

Manicures and pedicures

Everyone will be admiring your wedding ring so your hands should look as lovely as the rest of you. Treat yourself to a manicure to ensure your new band isn't let down by chewed nails and dry hands, and have a matching pedicure at the same time. Ask the manicurist if you can buy a bottle of whatever colour she applies so that you can take it on honeymoon with you. If you bite your nails, stop, even if it's for one month only. Coat your nails with the foul-tasting formulas that are available from chemists or ask a beauty therapist to apply acrylic tips to the ends. False nails have a tendency to flip off at inappropriate moments, so steer clear of them – you don't want to leave a pillar-box red talon behind when you're cutting the cake.

Hair and make-up to suit you

You want to look stunning, radiant, glamorous and beautiful on your wedding day, but remember you still want to look like you. Many brides get so carried away with strange ideas of what a bride should look like that they walk down the aisle and no-one recognises them. Work with a formula that you know looks good.

Make-up forever

If you don't normally wear much make-up, don't arrive at the church looking like a cheap transvestite. Wear a little more to enhance your best features and sample the new long-lasting brands to keep your make-up fresh for the photos, but don't go mad. Your fiancé will be terrified if he sees a painted ghoul hurrying towards him. Ask your mother or maid of honour to keep a waterproof mascara (you will cry at some point during the day – tears of laughter or sadness, hopefully, not regret) and your favourite lipstick in her handbag. That way, you can reapply whenever you need to. Investigate the new long-lasting, refreshing cosmetics on the market. If you've always dreamt of having someone else do your make-up, now is the time to indulge yourself. Make sure you have a run-through of colours and products at least a month before. Many freelance make-up artists now travel to the bride's home on the wedding day so check this out, and perhaps consider treating your mother and bridesmaids to a makeover too.

Hair today, gone tomorrow

A hairstyle is one of the quickest ways to age a bride. Just think back to all the bubble-permed brides of the seventies, or the Jennifer Aniston lookalikes of the nineties. Choose a cut and colour that suits you. Don't be too experimental. If something goes wrong, it can take a year to make it right. As soon as you get engaged, decide what you want to do and stick with it. Brides never did look good with paper bags over their heads. About three months before, start thinking about hair accessories and veils. Before the day, have a full run-through with your hairdresser to make sure that your chosen items look right with your hairstyle and can be pinned securely. Find a hairdresser who will travel to you on the morning of the wedding – this will eliminate unforeseen wind or rain disasters.

Secrets of Success

◆ Consider the time of year you are getting married. You may have always dreamt of wearing a fur-to-the-floor number, but in 90 degrees, you could arrive at the church looking like a stuffed pig. Vice versa, if you choose a mini dress on a day with an icy chill, you will show up looking (and feeling) like a frozen turkey. You can't predict exactly but be sensible.

◆ If you are unsure what style of dress suits you, try on as many different types as possible and take along a Polaroid camera to snap you in them. This way, you don't have to make any rash decisions and can ask people's opinions.

◆ Check the durability of your dress before you choose your accessories. You will be gutted if the carefully chosen lilies in your bouquet leave a nasty dust behind on your gown, or if the pots of bubbles you've given to your bridesmaids to blow over you and the groom for the pictures leave a gruesome green stain.

◆ Don't follow what the bridal fashion magazines say to the letter. They may insist that ballerina dresses are all the rage this season, but six months later they will be saying something completely different and you'll be immortalised as an over-grown Christmas fairy forever.

◆ On shopping trips, take along someone who you trust completely. Another pair of eyes will help when you are confronted with millions of styles. Make sure they are not easily bored – dress shopping is a drawn-out process. A clock-watcher will not endure this long ride.

◆ Do consider what the other members of the party will be wearing. If your groom is going modern, you really don't want to be dressed up like Anne Boleyn at a jousting tournament. If the bridesmaids are in cream, you really don't want to be wearing white (you'll make them look dirty). Stick to a complimentary, neutral shade.

◆ Remember just because you now look like a princess, you don't need to act like one. Brides who throw hysterical fits look pathetic. Despite what Elton John may think, tantrums and tiaras really don't mix. You look great and everyone knows it. Leave it at that.

◆ Pick shoes for style and comfort. You will be on your feet most of the day. Break them in by wearing them around the house (when your fiancé isn't around). If you can't find the perfect shade in a style that suits you, get them dyed to match. Most dressmakers and bridal shops can offer this as a service.

◆ Keep your dress a secret by hiding it at a friend's or relative's house. Don't keep it in those plastic dry-cleaning bags – they don't allow the fabric to breathe and the material can lose it's colour and shine. The best way to protect it is by covering it in clean, white bed sheets.

◆ Borrowing things will save you a small fortune. Call in the favours from past brides. One may have a lovely tiara or necklace, you may even find a dress which fits and has only been worn once.

◆ If your dress has beads or sequins, buy a small tube of fabric glue from a haberdashery store for emergency fixes on the day.

◆ Many brides change out of their dress and remove their veil in the evening. Why? This is your one chance to shine. If you intend to go mad on the dance-floor, pick a design that is easily adaptable with a removal train or a hook to gather up the skirts at your wrist.

- If you do opt for sensible thigh-grip, tummy-tuck tights, remove them before you go away with your new husband for the night. Practical they are. Sexy they're not.

- If you are having a dress made for you, ask the designer to draw and sign a sketch of it as a souvenir.

- If you are staying overnight at the reception venue, don't forget to pre-send an overnight bag. As much as you like your dress, you really don't want to wear it for breakfast the next morning. If you can afford a new going-away outfit, splash out, but don't worry if you can't. After a day in bridal paraphernalia, it's quite nice to slip into a pair of jeans and a T-shirt.

Chapter Six

Choosing a bridesmaid without upsetting all your female friends

However well women do at school, university, work, the Houses of Parliament or NASA, there's still a piece of each of us that would like to throw ourselves into an overgrown pink tutu and matching ballet pumps. Preferably with ribbon that wraps right round our calves stopping shortly before the knee. Okay, so by the time we've hit 18, most girls recognise that dancewear in holy places isn't a good look but you still want to try, because being a bridesmaid is cool. This is why you must think long and hard about whom you choose to ask. It will mean the world to the girls you pick but it could break the hearts of those you don't.

How many bridesmaids should you have?

A royal wedding party would be embarrassed by less than eight, but with the expense of a modern-day wedding, numbers have to be more realistic. One on her own can look a little odd and more than seven can look like a netball team, so go for anything in-between.

Who should you choose as your bridesmaids?

Friends as bridesmaids

Your friends will be the hardest to choose among. You will go from not wanting any bridesmaids to wanting twenty – just so they will all know how very important they are to you. Save time with this rather shallow but effective equation:

$$\frac{\text{Number of girlie holidays} \times \text{Years of friendship}}{\text{Number of arguments over the years}}$$

Once you have got a result, ring each one and ask if you can go out for a chat. When you do, she will have that expectant sound in her voice that all your female friends will develop when they hear you are engaged. Ask her face to face. It's surprisingly nerve-wracking, like asking someone out on a date, but really special too.

How to fine-tune your bridesmaid-from-hell detector

She may be your oldest friend but if you fight over where to go out for dinner, chances are she shouldn't be your chief bridesmaid. The last thing you need with all the other wedding worries is a stroppy bridesmaid refusing to wear your favoured style of shoe. If you have a friend who you feel you should ask but are worried about her behaviour, test the water first. Refer to past weddings, or even invent imaginary brides to find out her opinions on different things. If she openly states that all bridesmaids should have the final say in the dresses/hairstyles/hen night, then you know you can't trust her to go along with your wishes. The last thing a stressed-out bride needs is a bossy friend with a chip on her shoulder.

DEBORAH, 30

❝ My parents wanted to pay for my whole wedding, so this liberated me into thinking about asking lots of my friends to be bridesmaids. I decided to pick a friend from each part of my life, like a timeline of the girls I have shared a history with. That would mean having someone from junior school, high school, sixth form, university, my first job and my present job. I asked the six women and they were all thrilled and said yes straight away. But it wasn't until we got to arranging things that I realised I had made a really difficult situation for myself. Not only did the girls not know each other, but, to be honest, I didn't really know some of the girls myself anymore. Two of them had grown up to be such nightmares that I had to sack them just weeks before the wedding. I think I should have just stuck to one or two. ❞

Family members as bridesmaids

Choosing family members as bridesmaids can bring up a whole new set of problems: it's not just your wedding anymore, it belongs to the family *en masse*. As soon as you choose a sister or a cousin, that's it, it's not just a wedding, it's an excuse for a family knees-up because there are so many of you involved. And sometimes, for tradition's sake, you are asked to include people whom you really don't know. This can cause much resentment – especially if you have to choose them over your loyal, close friends.

Sisters
If you do have a sister, always ask her to be your bridesmaid first of all. Even if you aren't particularly close, it will save all the questions and arguments with your mother, and it could be the bonding event you've been waiting for all your lives. She may say no, thinking you should have your friends there to support you, but at least give her the option.

Cousins
If you want to ask any cousins, make sure it won't cause a major upset first. You can't ask one and not consider the others, especially if they are sisters. It would be easy just to pick the cutest/youngest one but the rest of the family may not approve. Also, before you choose, make sure they understand what you want. You must have either a good relationship with them, or, if they are under a certain age, with their mother. It's not enough to rely on a family bond.

The older generation
Some brides think it would be terribly cute to ask their mother or aunts to be their bridesmaids. It's not cute. It's creepy. Being a bridesmaid is for the under forties – and

that's being generous. Being followed up the aisle by a withered aunt may make you look better, and she may have been a great support to you throughout your life, but ask her daughter to be a flower girl or give her a special task instead. You don't want the congregation laughing – taffeta does nothing for mature skins.

DANIELLA, 27

❝ My mother basically told me whom I had to have as my bridesmaids: my three sisters. I would have asked them anyway, but my mother went ahead and told them they were doing it before I'd had a chance to speak to my fiancé – or my sisters – about it. I feel like I've been robbed of a special time that we could have shared now. And I'm sure my mother didn't ask them nicely like I had planned to do, she probably just barked instructions at them. Coming from Italian stock, family is extremely important and my mother sees herself as the powerhouse of the whole thing – like we'll fall apart without a strong matriarch. I guess I'm just lucky she didn't insist on all my distant relatives from Sicily singing in the church. Don't give in to family pressure over who should be your bridesmaids. If your best friend is closer to you than your sister, ask her or you'll always regret it. Just get some earplugs to deafen you to your mother's complaints. ❞

The dangers of asking children to be bridesmaids

Children fidget, involuntarily vomit and like rolling around on the floor in dirt. Why do you want young kids at your wedding again? They'll stick out their tongues in photos, scream during the important bits of the service and moan loudly about being bored during the speeches. But unfortunately, when it comes to bridesmaids, the younger they are, the cuter they are. If you want to borrow a tot for your big day, try to do the following: employ a chief bridesmaid who is good with kids or at least good at making them tow the line, make sure the mothers are behind you a hundred per cent when it comes to discipline and ask them to occupy the children. The happier and more entertained they are, the less likely they are to complain. Make girls between three and eight years old flower girls. That way they get to do the fun parts (sprinkle petals and throw confetti) but they are not required to stand with the bridal party for the entire ceremony. Don't dress them identically to the older girls either – this can look twee or tarty.

NB Page boys can be a pain too. Encourage them to look after the bridesmaids, distribute slices of wedding cake at the reception and behave themselves. If you have a lot of children attending the wedding, think about hiring an entertainer of some sorts. This keeps them quiet so the adults can get on and enjoy the day... and the evening.

What do you want your chief bridesmaid to do?

The number one priority of every maid of honour (matron of honour if she is married) should be looking after the bride. She should be your attendant, messenger and advisor. Times have changed and she does not have many formal responsibilities, she's there to lend moral support in the stressful months before the marriage. She's the person who restrains you when you want to punch your partner, and the friend whom you ring in the early hours of the morning when you are having a morality crisis. There are a few formal must-dos however:

A long time before the wedding

The chief bridesmaid's initial task is to help you choose your wedding dress and then to offer her thoughts on her own and the other bridesmaids' dresses and accessories. She should aid you by locating the perfect items and checking prices.

Closer to the wedding

Discuss the hen night with each other. Do you want your chief bridesmaid to plan everything or are you keen to have a say in what you get up to? If she is planning it all, remind her she'll need plenty of time and energy to plan the perfect event. Give her your other friends' phone numbers and emails so she can call them for inspiration and advice.

The night before the wedding

Mission control: your friend needs to keep you calm. Get her to stay the night with you if she can. She should be there to take your mind off the next day's events and keep you away from arguments with your parents. Go through a checklist together to make sure everything is okay. She should then answer any nagging doubts you have about life, death, the universe…

On the day

You'll need her to help you get into the dress for the ceremony. She should also make sure the other bridesmaids are behaving themselves. Ask her to carry emergency supplies in her handbag (tissues, waterproof mascara, tights etc.) or pass everything on to your mother. Throughout the day, she should help you to arrange your dress, train and veil, and hold your bouquet should you require her to. If you decide to change in the evening, your bridesmaid should accompany you and help you undress, promising to look after your wedding gown if you need her to.

What do the other bridesmaids do?

Traditionally, they help the chief bridesmaid to organise the bride and her hen night. Otherwise, they can help the bride's mother to organise the flowers, church and confetti. The older ones should look after the younger ones, and the younger ones' only responsibility is to look sweet and behave.

Sacking a bridesmaid

If you ask someone to be a bridesmaid but then it doesn't work out, try to talk things through calmly and logically. It's hard to stop emotion running wild with anything to do with weddings. If she doesn't soften her stance and start supporting you more, tell her where to get off – at the first bus stop outside of Bridesmaidsville. You could lose a friend or you could be doing her a favour in the long run – you'll have to decide which will be the best and calmest solution for you.

How to dress your bridesmaids

When it comes to dressing bridesmaids there are two kinds of bride. Name and definition to follow:

Kind Bride

She is confident that she will be the belle of the ball, regardless of how slim/sexy/stunning her bridesmaids are. She is also content that even if her best friend is a rounded Russian shot-putter with a full-grown beard, she will not ruin the official photographs – despite protestations from an increasingly dictatorial mother. So what Kind Bride does is think about what colours are likely to suit her bridesmaids' skin tones and what style of sleeve will cover bingo wings. There are different scales of Kind Brides. Moderate ones take their bridesmaids with them on dress shopping trips and declare the wedding a no-bow-and-lace area. (All brides-to-be, please note: bows never did anyone any good.) Next are the Kind Brides who actually choose a style to suit their bridesmaids' shapes and agree to pay for alterations wherever they are needed. Finally, the Kindest Bride of all is the one who agrees that her assorted attendants can wear varying shades and styles of dress to suit all their needs. This bride wants her helpers to be happy.

Cruel Bride

She has waited for this day all her life. Cruel Bride will stand out. She will have the best wedding ever. It will be an aesthetic affair to remember. So, by these definitions alone, she is torn. She needs to look a hundred times better than any other woman in the room (and with the stylish, affordable range of Phillip Treacy wedding hats now available at

Marks & Spencer, she is already wary of the competition from the congregation). So to have her bridesmaids in chic, classic little dresses and fashionable tiaras could be too much. She could self-explode. She wants her wedding to be the cream of the crop, so she can't put her chosen friends in potato sacks (the possibility had crossed her mind), but she doesn't have to pay much attention to their likes or dislikes. For Cruel Bride, bows are definitely an option.

NB Cruel brides should also remember the old superstition, 'three times a bridesmaid never a bride'. Is there an old friend you particularly dislike? Would you like to see her end up as a wizened old prune of a spinster? If she's already been a bridesmaid twice, go for it!

Who should pay for the bridesmaids' dresses?

Normally, the bride pays for the bridesmaids' dresses, especially if they are never to be worn again. The cost of accessories is normally taken care of by the bridesmaids themselves, or by their parents if they are children. If the bride and bridesmaids have discussed buying dresses which can be worn again and that are a little more expensive than planned, the bridesmaids should expect to share the financial burden. Traditionally, the ushers pay for their own outfits, so there is no reason why the girls can't help out too.

Is a wedding a wedding without bridesmaids?

You don't need to have bridesmaids at all. The traditional duties of a maid or matron of honour can easily be handed to your sister or mother. The cost is a big factor in not having any bridesmaids. By the time you have paid for dresses, accessories, bouquets and hairdressing, you may start to resent them if they are not very thankful. One option is to make people attendants rather than bridesmaids. This means they wear their own outfits; you just supply them all with matching, beautiful bouquets and have a few special portraits taken. This is a good idea if you have lots of older women who you would like to include but who would look a bit silly traipsing behind you in matching gowns.

How to compensate the disappointed

Letting down your expectant family and friends won't be as difficult as you imagine. You can give the runners-up their own special tasks to do to soften the blow of unbridesmaid-edness.

Readings during the ceremony

Ask your friends to give special readings during your ceremony. Many people think readings have to be religious – they don't. Ask a friend to choose something that reflects your friendship: a poem you studied together at school or the lyrics to your favourite song at university (if it's appropriate, no Iron Maiden). If you know your friend can write well, how about asking her to compose a special message for you and the groom – this way she can reflect everything about you, and her feeling towards you? She can make it funny, sad or sentimental, the choice is hers. If your reader is stuck, spend a day together going through books of poetry and prose. Most ceremonies have between one to three readings so make the most of this. Remember though, it can be a daunting experience, so choose confident friends who you know would be comfortable doing this.

Musical accompaniment

Perhaps you have a friend who can sing or play an instrument very well. Ask them to perform either before you arrive at the venue or while you are signing the register. Not only will they get to show off their amazing talent, but also you can commemorate their performance by adding their name and performance to the order of service.

Witnesses

Every couple needs two people to witness the wedding formalities and to sign their marriage licence. Traditionally, the two fathers are given this role. But as dads will have enough to do, how about passing this honour to other people who would like to be involved in some way. Check with your parents first – especially if they are quite old-fashioned – but if they don't mind, think of some friends who would take the matter seriously and respectfully. The photographer will snap them signing their name and the registrar will shake their hand, sealing their own special part in your wedding history.

Special helpers

Some friends don't want to play a big part in a ceremony, if they are essentially shy or quiet. If they don't know lots of the other people involved, being a bridesmaid, reader or witness could be quite daunting. So ask them to do special jobs for you that only they could get right – and then reward them with a special gift and a thank you during the groom's speech. Ask an artistic friend to design the table plan, or ask an eager seamstress to help you perfect your dress. They will relish the opportunity of being involved behind the scenes while taking a back seat on the day itself.

When there just aren't enough jobs for everyone

There will still be some people left over, of course, thinking they stood an outside chance of having a role at the wedding. So just make sure you take them aside at one point, either at the wedding or at the hen night, and tell them how important it is for you that they are going to watch you go from Miss to Mrs and that you really value their friendship. It sounds a bit calculated to point this out, but you won't regret doing it. Wedding or no wedding, we probably don't tell the people we love often enough how special they are to us. A wedding is a good excuse to blame it on the alcohol or hormones and explain to them what they mean to you. Some friends would make better Godparents or legal guardians anyway, so pencil them on to your mental list for your next life-changing event.

Wedding-day angels

Despite the hassles, there is a reason why the custom of having bridesmaids has lasted so long: when you are about to walk into that church and the vicar is preaching ominously and your mother is flapping around you, it's nice just to look around on lots of smiley, proud faces, telling you how lucky you are to have found such a great man. You know that they will do anything to help you in return for this special badge of honour. Just make sure you choose the right ones.

Secrets of Success

◆ When asking someone to be your chief bridesmaid, be sensible. You may have known her since you were knee-high to a grasshopper but are there aspects of her personality you know wouldn't work? If she is selfish/a bad timekeeper /maniacally depressed/a man hater/a fashion nazi... asking her could be more trouble than it's worth. If you do want to reward her friendship (why are you friends with someone like this anyway?) then set out the guidelines as soon as you ask her.

◆ Do think ahead to the hen night. Do you trust the person that will have to make all the decisions, if not, change the rules and organise it yourself? The chief bridesmaid may be grateful to have the pressure taken off her anyway.

◆ Think back to when you were a kid, and try to make your wedding as magical and fairy-taleish as possible for the under elevens. Think back to when you were a teenager and remember how embarrassing and uncool everything was, so make your adolescents feel like they're helping you plan a big party. Think back to when you were choosing your wedding dress. You didn't like frou-frou and pastel pink so why would your grown-up bridesmaids? It is your day but it is they're reputations at stake. Dress them in something you would be happy to wear yourself and you can't go wrong.

◆ Do remember though, that it is ultimately your day, and if one of your chosen attendants is out of line, take it up with her.

Explain that you have enough stress with all the other arrangements and that you picked her because you knew she would be supportive and easy-going and make you laugh when everything else was going wrong. That should get her on your side again.

♦ Ask your bridesmaids not to smoke during the ceremony and photos. You'd think they wouldn't need to be asked, but some have been known to light up as soon as they leave the church. Nothing ruins the look like a packet of Benson & Hedges and a hovering cloud of smoke. In the same vein – ask them not to drink excessively until after the speeches and to wear knickers. Again, you wouldn't think you'd need to ask but...

♦ And last but not least, to all you bridesmaids-to-be, just in case you're reading this. Planning a wedding is a nightmare. Paying for it is a nightmare. You may think you are one of the most important people involved – and you are – but don't act like a movie star. If she wants you to wear flat shoes, don't refuse and show up in three-inch stilettos. Just do it. Having a bridesmaid costs a small fortune (dress, shoes, head decoration, flowers, hairdresser, make-up artist and gift) and most brides will admit that they are doing it more for other people than themselves. So keep it real. Accept the honour and all the strange choices that come with it and prepare to be a beauty queen for the day.

Chapter Seven

Balancing being a wedding bore with a full-time job

THE TROUBLE WITH brides-to-be is that they have a one-track mind. As soon as they get an engagement ring on their finger, all thoughts of work and play go out of the window. Unless of course it is work and play relating to the wedding. Most brides turn into Bridezillas: strange and dangerous creatures who are obsessively demanding over plans for their big day. Some Bridezillas have become so deranged they have banned guests from their reception for being too fat or ugly. Don't let this happen to you. No one likes an aggressive wedding bore, and, believe me, no one likes a wedding bore less than a boss with an office to run.

Announcing your good news to your colleagues

Telling your fellow workers your good news can lead to a variety of responses because they don't love you like your family and friends do. The ex-brides will sincerely wish you well but then distance themselves. They remember all too clearly how much they leaned on their colleagues during the run-up to their big day and they don't fancy filling in for you over the summer. The romantics will get flushed with excitement and be at your side until the wedding. If there's a crisis, they will want to sort it out, if there's an urgent message, they will want to take it and, most importantly, if there's an opportunity to go shoe shopping in your lunch hour, they will want to go with you. Romantics can be useful so don't be too sensitive about allotting them a few

---

KATE, 26

❝ I decided that I was going to let the time go quietly past at work until my wedding day without making 'too much of it', however my work friends decided otherwise. When people at work asked me about the wedding I would quickly give a run down of where I was with it all, but quite frankly the more I spoke about the wedding the more it bored me. So I thought about the impact it must have had on other people! However, there is a hard balance to strike at work as one doesn't want to appear a bore, but then they don't want to appear like they are not excited either. ❞

tasks. The men in the office will offer congratulations and then pretend nothing has changed. If the man is married, he'll remember how delirious all women seem to get before matrimony, and if he isn't, your wedding will remind him of his girlfriend/lack of girlfriend and will send him into a state of panic about his future and being tied down.

Beware of career women's rejection of marriage

Not every woman wants to get married. Some consider it old-fashioned, hypocritical and pointless. A few women were told somewhere along the line that you can't have both a happy marriage and a brilliant career, so they made their choice and a career seemed the more appealing option. They work long hours, even Christmas holidays, and think married women are silly and irrelevant. They probably live on their own and have a cat. Beware of this type of woman. If she has made a conscious decision to be on her own, there may be a lot of resentment. She may regret it now and feel that it is too late. She will probably try to make you feel weak, foolish and irresponsible with a few feminist asides. Try to take them in your stride.

NB You should control your wedding exuberance when in the company of divorcees, widows and those who are unlucky in love. No one likes a smug show-off, and a newly engaged woman could come across as one. With friends and family, you know their stories and what is acceptable. In a work environment, people's private lives should remain private, so think before you speak.

Why is the boss scared of your future domestic bliss?

Statistics show that workers who are content in long-term relationships spend less time at the office and are not as enthusiastic about overtime or business socialising as their single counterparts. Your boss may assume that your imminent marriage signals an end to your extra hours and 'work first, home life second' mentality.

DIANA, 40

❝ You'd think that in the 21st century, women could get married – as men do – and resume their successful careers. Not so! As soon as I returned from honeymoon, I noticed the partners making assumptions and jokes about my new marital status. Only silly things, like I wouldn't be able to entertain clients anymore because I had to rush home to cook my husband's dinner, but I was offended. I now feel like I have to work twice as hard as my married, male colleagues, to gain the same respect. Especially because they assume I'm going to rush off to breed any day because I'm in my forties. They don't seem to believe that I want a career more than a child. ❞

Why are newly-weds expected to get pregnant immediately?

When you return to the office after your honeymoon, you'll notice a change straight away. Assuming that marriage means you want to have children, your male and more mature female colleagues will ask, 'When will we hear the patter of tiny feet?' on a regular basis. Sad but true, many industrial dinosaurs still think that having babies is a woman's ultimate task. They assume any pretence at a career is a mere filler before she turns to her natural vocation of childbearing. If you want to have children soon after marriage, go for it, but be aware of the incorrect, but nevertheless, harmful effect it might have on your career. Maternity benefits and childcare are improving but there's still a lot of work to do.

> **NB When you do decide to have children,** before or after you are married, weigh up who should take time off after the birth to look after baby. The responsibility shouldn't automatically fall to the woman, especially if she has a more promising, rewarding and financially beneficial career than her partner.

How can you organise your wedding from the office?

1. Use your lunch hour wisely. Instead of heading to the canteen for a gossip, sit at your desk while it's quiet and make a plan of action, go through your diary to check appointments or update your lists. If you work flexitime, work straight through so you can leave an hour early. This will be handy when you've got to rush to shops and venues before they shut.

2. Use the amenities subtly. As long as you don't leave a huge folder on your desk, marked WEDDING FILE, you can probably get away with making the occasional phone call or giving out your email address to your suppliers. Most people don't have fax machines at home so give out the

work's fax number – just make sure you're standing by the fax when it comes through. If you get on well with your boss, check this is all okay and cut down on all other personal messages.

3. Call in the professionals. If you work with anyone that could be useful to you, ask him or her for help. Offer them payment of course, but you can offer them less than people that specialise in the wedding market. Look out for designers, caterers, photographers, chauffeurs, hair-dressers etc.

4. Use time while commuting. Unless you're driving to work, plan your day while travelling to work. Read up on your wedding books and magazines rather than the daily news. You might become astoundingly ignorant but you'll feel calm about your wedding.

Getting married within your holiday entitlement

As soon as you have the wedding date, book in the few sur-rounding days either side as vacation. If you leave it too late, someone else may have booked their holiday, which will lead to guilt, resentment and expense on both sides.

Many companies have a policy that employees can only take a maximum of two weeks off at a time. For weddings and honeymoons, an exception is generally made, so speak to your boss or the personnel department before you panic. If you are worried about not having enough holiday entitle-ment, speak to the people in the know and see if you can carry days forward from the previous year. Many large firms also allow you to buy back holiday if there is a special reason. Signing your life away definitely counts as a special reason.

If you are worried about taking all your holiday, think about getting married on a Bank Holiday weekend or over Christmas, when you will have spare days allotted to you anyway.

Learning when to prioritise

If things can wait, let them wait. You shouldn't panic about things that can be left till the weekend. The office should really only be used for urgent, life-threatening tasks like signing and faxing your wedding insurance form.

Learning when to deputise

You don't have to do it all yourself. Now is the time to take advantage of enthusiastic parents who are retired or house-keepers. Issue them all with clear instructions and enough money to cover costs and they can take the strain. The same goes for your partner – just because he's male it doesn't mean he's florally illiterate. If you have a secretary or assistant at work who is as excited about the wedding as you, s/he may also be keen to help out. Just don't overstep the professional line. This could cause problems in the long run.

Learning when to shut up

Your wedding isn't the be all and end all for everyone. Just for you and your mother. In general, people will be happy for you and then they'll forget about it. It's not that they are rude, insensitive or jealous, just that they have their own lives. Especially in the workplace, the only reason you spend time together is to make money for the business. Don't become such a wedding bore that you are excluded from important meetings or social events because people assume your brain has turned to mush. If you see people hiding in filing cabinets or under tables, that is a clue to shut up.

The wedding invitation as networking tool

It may seem a good idea to invite your boss, important customers and influential team members to your wedding. You may hope that your hospitality and popularity make you appear attractive for promotion – and they might be good for an expensive gift. Just remember that the day will fly by without you having a chance to speak to even your nearest and dearest. If you think inviting work people will take up more of your time than you can afford, don't invite them. Most people hate attending weddings when they don't know the bride and groom as a couple anyway. And your good idea may backfire: they may assume you haven't got enough friends and are trying to keep numbers up with acquaintances. Stick to inviting your work friends and don't invite to impress.

Should you change to your married name?

Privately it is up to you and your partner to decide what you should do. Many couples keep their own names until the birth of the first child, when the woman takes the man's name so the family are the same. If you have built up a name for yourself professionally, there is no problem in keeping one name for the office and one name for home. It may get a little confusing when you're signing or paying for things, but it will stop contacts and headhunters getting confused. Of course, if you have developed into a terrible wedding bore, change your name as soon as you are married, find a new job and hopefully everyone will treat you like a new, efficient human being again.

Secrets of Success

◆ Don't hold off doing any professional qualifications or courses until after the wedding – you may not be offered them again. If you have to cope, you will and it may help you keep things in perspective.

◆ People aren't stupid. If you start taking regular sickies before the day, your boss will assume you are not ill and just bunking off to organise things. He'll remember this until the day you leave the firm.

◆ If you don't have the space or money to invite work friends, suggest a lunch out the week before. It will give you the chance to let your hair down and involve your colleagues in the excitement.

◆ If invitations get a bit political, think about just inviting everybody to the evening reception. You can't leave only one or two people out so this is the cheapest way of doing it.

◆ Due to the nature of a working relationship, colleagues will probably not mind attending your wedding on their own, even if they are married themselves. As long as they know other people there, they will treat it as a work night out rather than a family knees-up. The women in accounts may even prefer to leave their old men at home.

Chapter Eight

How to avoid killing your parents

PARENTS: YOUR ROCK in times of need. Your friends when others desert you. Your first call in a case of emergency. Yep, maybe, but get that engagement ring on your finger and mention the word 'wedding' and they turn into strange creatures. Is it a panicky reaction to the well-documented expense of a family wedding? Or is it the nostalgic disbelief that their baby girl is flying the nest (metaphorically of course, you probably left home years ago)? Whether it's either of these things, or something else altogether, parents go nuts. You may love them as normal, rational, easy-going folk but prepare yourself for a major change. You'll want to kill them. They'll want to kill you. Just make sure they don't kill your chances of a dream wedding.

How to solve your parents' attitude problem

PROBLEM: disinterested parents

These mothers and fathers act as though your marriage to the man of your dreams doesn't interest them. They act like it doesn't affect them or, even worse, that it was always so obvious that you were going to marry this particular chap that they can't see why you want to make such a big fuss about it. They don't understand that you are not making a big fuss, you just want them to act like 'normal' parents and be happy for you. Maybe insist they put an engagement announcement in the local paper or throw you a little soirée to celebrate your good news? Don't be silly. Disinterested parents will listen to you sharing your news about the proposal and they will try to feign interest in the ring but soon enough, you will notice their eyes glaze over at the mere mention of the word 'wedding'. As soon as you take a breather, they are animatedly back to discussing Johnny Fairweather from the golf club or their next trip to Tenerife. Unfortunately girls, it seems they would rather discuss the price of Brussels sprouts than your big day. Selfish creatures.

Solution

Try to accept your parents for what they are: selfish adults like everyone else on the planet. When you were a child, the world stopped turning when you were ill or unhappy. Now you're grown-up and away from them, they've had to make sure it doesn't. You've got new friends and interests – a new life – that you find more interesting than theirs, and they've developed a new life too. But tell them you are upset by their lack of interest and see what they do. Ask them to take a break from all the wonderful plans they've got for next year to offer you some advice. They will be flattered that their dynamic, modern child still needs them. If they are still disinterested after your chat, sulk, scream and then admit that it's probably better if they don't interfere. You'd only end up holding the reception at the golf club with Johnny Fairweather as DJ if they had.

JOANNE, 26

❛ Simon and I announced our engagement after just four months of dating and just a couple of visits to the parents. We both have close relationships with our parents but they probably didn't know how serious we were about each other and so our good news probably came as quite a shock. To begin with, my parents were very reluctant to discuss anything and then as the time got closer, there did seem to be a bit of friction between what they wanted and what we wanted. Basically, my parents seemed concerned about the expense of it all and so whilst I was busy thinking along the lines of a castle, they were thinking more of the village hall. So I sat down with them and explained that Simon and I had been putting money aside for the wedding and therefore we didn't expect them to contribute any more than they felt comfortable with. Secondly, we compromised on the castle and decided on a lovely country hotel instead. ❜

PROBLEM: budget-conscious parents

They are worried about the money. Their friends' daughter got married last year and it crippled them for six months. Your parents have dreams of paying off the mortgage and going on a cruise. How can they tell you that they can't pay for such an expensive day?

Solution

They don't realise that you want to pay for half/the majority of the wedding with your partner. They assume that things are the same as when they got married. Back then, the bride's family was expected to pay for everything. Fill them in on the new methods of saving and planning a wedding. Don't show up at their house with elaborate brochures and menus. Your dad will feel embarrassed. Make it clear that any contribution they make will be more than you expected (which may or may not be the truth) and thank them wholeheartedly.

PROBLEM: anti-ageing parents

In their eyes, you are still five years old and attending ballet classes. They don't like the fact you are sleeping with this man, and now they don't like the fact that all their friends are going to know about it. Anyway, aren't you supposed to be daddy's girl? In his eyes, you getting married means he is no longer the number-one man in your life and he's right, isn't he? For your mother, it is a sign that she is getting old. Having a daughter old enough to get married is the ultimate sign of being over the hill.

Solution

Now is the time to lay the affection on thick. Remind your dad of all the fun you had when you were kids, and throw in the promise of grandchildren at some stage. This always softens up parents (they get the cute kid without the responsibility), and takes their minds off the problems at hand. Spend some extra time with your mum, tell her how attractive she still is, and persuade her to try some new make-up colours or a new hairstyle. Remind them you are still their little girl by leaving dirty plates and knickers around the house and sulking on a regular basis. They'll soon be grateful someone's taking you off their hands.

PROBLEM: serious parents

They are intelligent, mature adults. Just because their daughter is getting hitched it doesn't mean they have suddenly to start showing an unhealthy interest in flowers, cakes, dresses and romance, does it? All this fluffy, frou-frou stuff can be too much for a middle-aged couple. Your dad would rather let the frivolity take place in another room. He's always thought you were a bit soppy and emotional anyway and the detail you are paying to such trivial matters only proves his point. Your mum just thinks it's all a bit OTT and expensive. When she got married it was a registry office, a few curly ham sandwiches and a honeymoon in Cornwall. She thinks modern girls have gone gaga over weddings.

Solution
Have they got a point? Are you turning into the Sugar Plum Fairy? Are you buzzing around florists like Liberace on speed? Maybe you should keep a lid on it. Weddings shouldn't take over your life 24/7. Make time to plan and prepare, and, during the rest of the time, try to have normal, adult conversations. Believe it or not, the economy

is slightly more important than your silk slippers. Only just, but get a grip and your parents will come round.

PROBLEM: divorced parents

They've been through a messy divorce. Sure, they've come through the other side (eventually) but it's tainted their outlook on marriage. Your mother has reservations about all men. It didn't work for her so why should it work for you? In her eyes, you are young and silly – just like she was when she married your father – and about to make the same giant mistake she did. She can't put a mask on and pretend she thinks it's all okay. The wounds of love have scarred her for life. Your father just thinks it's a bag of old nonsense which doesn't help anyone. He keeps reminding you that one-third of marriages now end in divorce, so why bother?

Solution

Try to understand their feelings. You were hurt by their divorce so it will be ten times worse for them. They were once young, positive and in love, like you are now. Be sympathetic, but at the same time force them to accept that this is a fresh start, a new beginning. You are not the same as them and you won't make the same mistakes. You're not saying that marriage suits everyone and that you are going to live happily ever after. But you're going to give it a shot and you really need their support.

NB Divorced parents can also cause a lot of difficulties with the formal wedding arrangements.

KATE, 29

❝ My parents divorced five years ago and hate each other, so my wedding was a nightmare. Initially, they both refused to go if the other was invited because they couldn't promise not to start fighting. I offered to place them at different ends of the room, but they rebuffed me. One month before the event, I sent them both invites and they did come – although they ignored each other. The fact that they were so spitefully disinterested in something so important to me hurt immeasurably and I'm not sure I'll ever be able to forgive them. ❞

PROBLEM: he's-not-good-enough-for-our-daughter parents

They don't like your fiancé. Parents – as we all know – have a sixth sense about people, and mothers in particular can hear warning bells a mile off. They might have noticed something sinister in his behaviour towards you, he may have been rude to your siblings, and he may even have come on to your mum in the kitchen on Christmas Day.

Solution

If you suspect they're not keen on your man, ask them for evidence of misdemeanours. Either you will discover something that you should know before you are legally bound to him, or you'll be able to discredit their theories and hopefully win them over. Some parents will never think that anyone is good enough for their child and we just have to learn to accept it. If the comments continue after your chat, make a stand. Don't say that it's him or your parents, but make it clear how important he is to you and how they are upsetting you.

> **NB It's worse when your parents actually prefer** your spouse to their own child and thank him for taking you off their hands.

PROBLEM: scared parents

Your relationship hasn't been brilliant over the years: you've had emotional ups and downs (especially when your mother was pre-menstrual and you were pre-pubescent) and they're not completely sure where they stand with you. They don't want to act too chummy and interested in case you think they're interfering. These parents are petrified of you. Your mother is desperate to go dress shopping with you but suspects you'd rather take your friends. Your father wants to get to know your fiancè but thinks you are always too busy.

Solution

Only you can sort out this situation. Have you had a historically bad relationship with your parents? Have you told them to leave you alone, refused to let them enter your bedroom and just grunted in response to questions about your career/love life and friends? If so, you've got some serious mending to do. They are annoying, especially when you just want some peace and quiet after a busy day in the office, but they love you. Let them back into your life – and your wedding – slowly but surely, and you might find that your wedding can solve all the problems you have had in the past. Sharing new memories as adults can help to erase the difficulties of the past.

PROBLEM: over-enthusiastic parents

Your mother is so enthusiastic she thinks she is the bride. She daydreams of flowers and the 'Wedding March', she giggles girlishly while flicking through the latest issue of *Wedding and Home*. Over-enthusiastic dads are normally trying to impress their friends from the pub/office/golf club/gym. This is why your small, carefully selected guest list expands to lots of strangers as soon as your parents get their hands on it.

Solution

Perhaps they just want the biggest and the best for their little girl. Look at it from your parents' point of view. There aren't too many excuses for a big get together with the relatives any more, and this is their chance to show how well you are all doing, especially if you are the only daughter. It is your day first and foremost, but let them share in the excitement for an easy life.

> **NB If you are one of five girls,** however enthusiastic your father might be on the inside, he's more likely to pat you on the back, wish you well and offer you £100 to put behind the bar. In this era of big weddings, life has never been harder for a man with lots of female children.

PROBLEM: super-planner parents

What starts off as a helping hand soon develops into a patriarchal mode of fascism. A pre-wedding mother could give Hitler a run for his money. She might as well be dressed in camouflage gear and called sergeant for the amount of swift, military manoeuvres she's going to try and pull off before your big day. But what a super-planner mother doesn't understand is that her idea of the best wedding ever might not be yours.

Solution

Before you have opened your first issue of *Bliss For Brides*, she is there, with a 'to do' list as long as her arm, barking instructions at your hopeless dad, and making your husband-to-be regret ever trying to make an honest woman of you. To pacify her, pass on the tasks that you really don't care about (ordering the cars etc.) but keep special things aside for you and your partner to plan. Threaten to elope, and the thought of such disruption and disorder will keep them on the right track.

HEIDI, 32

❝ I am a grown woman, with a good career, my own flat and a successful relationship. So why my parents thought that when it came to planning my own wedding, I would be a complete disaster, I don't know. To say my mother took over the reins would be an understatement – and my dad was just as bad. About six months before the day, my fiancé and I went away on holiday for a week. A few arrangements hadn't been made yet but we were in control and happy with the situation. When we got back, my mother had shoved a letter through the door with a list of things she'd done on it – ordering the church flowers, inviting her extended family and hiring a string quartet. So my dream wedding was spoilt by my parents' bossiness. These things still niggle me. Whatever you do, set out guidelines of what you want straight away. ❞

The displacement theory

A lot of the time, when you argue with your parents, you are not mad at them, you are displacing your anger. When you should be screaming at caterers, florists and other idiots, you scream at you parents instead. This is because you know that they will love you unconditionally and tell you the truth. You can rely on your parents for these two things more than your partner. Parents are irritating, but after the wedding you'll wonder what all the arguing was about.

How can your partner help?

My parents were super-planners. They left Jennifer Lopez's efforts in the shade. No job was too big, no task too difficult. My mum dedicated a special compartment in her filing cabinet to the event and wrote in her diary when things needed to be paid for. My fiancé found this sweet; I found it slightly annoying. He thought they were being generous; I sensed an ulterior motive. This is where partners can help. They have no baggage and can judge a situation at face value. You are carrying resentments and prejudice from early childhood. Always speak to your partner before jumping to conclusions.

Men are also slightly calmer about weddings than women. A sweeping generalisation, but that's because it's true. My mother hung up on me twice and I called her a bitch once. My fiancé and dad got together and sorted out the finer details over a few beers. Much more civilised. So take advantage of your partner's hormonal balance and ask him to go into the wedding war zone when you know you'll scream, cry or swear.

The in-laws

Just when you think that one set of parents is enough, along comes a new set: desperate to get involved (even if not financially) and desperate to offer their advice. A mother-in-law can be even worse than your mother because you don't share the same genetic tastes and intimacy. In fact all you share is the love for her son – and the fact that he has another woman in his life may have put her nose out of joint already. Don't listen to her silly talk about ex-con-quests (your partner has filled you in on this already) and don't let her compare your wedding to her daughter's/own/sister's. Keep her informed, keep it friendly but keep her at a distance, unless your mother is completely disinter-ested and then you can use her as a surrogate.

> **NB However annoying your mother-in-law is,** your partner won't be able to see it. He thinks the sun shines out of her bottom. So keep your criticisms to yourself unless they are serious. It won't do your relationship any favours and it's bound to get back to her one day.

Money

Parents shout too much, gossip too much, criticise too much and shake their heads too much. Brides-to-be often look at me like I'm mad when I say this. They say that their mothers have made promises not to interfere: 'My mother's not like that.' They all start like this: 'She said, she'll only help out where I need her and that she doesn't expect any kind of return on her time or financial investment.' Don't believe a word of it. These promises aren't worth the wind they're spoken on. For every pound your parents donate to the wedding fund, or hour they spend on the phone to a caterer, they'll want a pound of the action in return. You have to decide whether you need the money and help that badly, or whether you want to gain full control.

Are you really such a modern girl?

You might think so until you realise that being a traditional girl means mummy and daddy pick up the bill for a lot more. Traditionally, the bride and groom get off easy as costs are divided into three categories, the most expensive belonging to the bride's parents.

Parents of the brides' expenditure

- The reception (venue, food, entertainment, drinks and decorations)
- Transport for the bride and all her attendants to the church and reception
- Flowers for the bride, her attendants, the church and reception
- Invitations and postage
- Photographer and video-maker
- Insurance
- Press announcements

The groom's expenditure

◆ The wedding rings

◆ Buttonholes for himself, attendants and congregation

◆ His outfit (the ushers should pay for their own)

◆ Gifts for the attendants

◆ The honeymoon

◆ The church or register office fees, including extras such as choir and bellringers

The bride's expenditure

◆ Bridesmaids' dresses and accessories

◆ Bridal gown and accessories

◆ Hair and make-up for herself and attendants

But for the last ten years or so, modern couples have been taking a lot more of the responsibility, and paying for the bulk of the ceremony and party themselves. A father often feels it is his duty (and honour) to pay for his daughter's wedding, and, if he hasn't got much money, it can cause major heartache. If you know this is the case, just ask him to pay for things that he is particularly interested in that won't break the bank, such as the rock 'n' roll band you've hired for the evening or the cocktails you are going to serve as people enter the dining room. This way he will feel involved and useful without having to sell his home and move into a caravan.

Secrets of Success

◆ Remember this is your marriage you're planning, and not just a party; always put your partner's needs before your parents. People say there are two people in a marriage. Well, in a wedding there are three: the bride, her mother and her father. If you're not careful, you'll get so carried away in planning with your parents that you'll forget to ask how your partner feels about something. Just because he is being quiet and laid-back and not moaning and caterwauling like your parents, doesn't mean he is any less interested. He's probably just a bit more mature. Also remember, however wonderful it might be for you that your father has offered to pick up the bulk of the bill, your partner is a man in his own right and his pride could be taking a blow. He might want to provide the perfect day for the love of his life so make sure you discuss your parents' financial input with him too.

◆ You are the key to a happy wedding. As well as keeping your partner happy, you have to remember that it is a very important day for your parents too. Anyone who has walked down the aisle with her father will know this (my father has never smiled so brightly in his life – he insists it is the best day he has ever had). Make a big deal out of staying with your parents the night before the wedding; tell them how nice it is to be home for one last time. Insist your dad gives a speech – some nervous fathers may pretend they don't want to – so that all your friends can see how great he is. And pick a quiet moment at the reception to tell them how much you love them both. Don't take the easy option and give your mother a bunch of flowers, think of something personal that you know she would love – a beautiful handbag, vouchers for a facial, a compilation of her favourite songs. Something that

lets her know you've thought about her as a person, not just
another wedding chore to organise.

♦ Try to remember your in-laws. Everyone assumes the parents
of the bride are the only ones who matter but just because a
mother has a son, it doesn't mean she doesn't care about
who he ends up with or what kind of a wedding he has. Buy
your new mother-in-law a special present too, and make time
during the reception for her to show you off proudly to all her
friends and relatives. Make a friend of your mother-in-law as
soon as possible, it will save you lots of potential trouble in
the future.

♦ If you really can't bear the thought of your parents having a
say in your wedding to any degree, say no to all offers of
money. It will be tough, you may have to have a longer
engagement and/or a smaller wedding but it will save lots of
trouble in the future. You may not do things how they would
like them to be done, but at least your parents will never be
able to complain that they wasted their money on the wedding or that you didn't consider their feelings enough.

♦ Give your parents a break – they are not superhuman, unfortunately they are only human, just like you and I. So as hard
as it is, understand why your parents are angry, jealous,
envious or sad and treat them how you would like to be
treated yourself – as an adult. Weddings have changed so
much over the last few generations that they may need gentle
coaching on new wedding styles.

Chapter Nine

The hen night – a bride-to-be's road to ruin

IT'S NOT JUST IN THE workplace that women are taking over the world. Go to any town centre on a Saturday night and you'll see a gaggle of girls, looking gorgeous and feeling foxy. No doubt they are on a modern girl's hen night, leaving the men indoors while they paint the town red.

Why do we have hen nights?

Hen nights never used to be like they are today. It's only been in the last thirty years or so that they have become synonymous with sex toys and alcohol. Admittedly they have been around for a long time (historians claim they started around the time of Charles II in the 17th century), but when they began they were quiet affairs held in the brides' family homes. The women would get together and examine the contents of her 'bottom drawer', a treasure chest crammed with items the couple would need for their new home, and maybe enjoy a cup of tea, laced with tea.

In Victorian times, things got a little racier; the bride would meet with her mother and grandmother to talk about the facts of life. Girls didn't know about anything remotely sexual until they were married in those days. Well, that was the plan anyway – some of the unmarried ones still managed to get pregnant. Over the last century, things got a little crazier still. There might be a bottle of champagne to go round a group of 12, or they might sneakily look at posters of Montgomery Clift and James Dean in a lustful manner. But it wasn't until the seventies, the decade that taste forgot but sleaze remembered, that women and their hen nights started to give the men a run for their money.

The hen night becomes the hen week

Today, hen nights have grown from a couple of Babychams and a stripper at a local restaurant to weekends in capital cities, and sometimes even two weeks in the Caribbean, Bali or the Seychelles. This is fine if you are all investment bankers with a big-time bonus coming up, but I suspect you're not. Historically, this could be your last girlie holiday (although modern married girl's are increasingly taking vacations alone or *en masse*) so you want it to be special. But with the right guests and the right mood, it can be great wherever you choose to hold it. It doesn't need to be on a beach as far away from the groom as possible.

If you are dead set on a certain hen night that no one else will be able to afford, think about subsidising the trip. Limit the numbers to closest friends and you may be able to have the wildest hen night in the world – and your friends will think you are the coolest. Budget this into your wedding planner from the beginning and you won't even notice the missing cash.

TARA, 30

❝ I don't get to see my girlfriends very often so I was looking forward to my hen weekend a great deal. I chose a spa hotel that was central, so that no one would have more than three hours to travel, and gave everyone four months' notice. I couldn't believe the response I got. I've never heard so many pathetic excuses for non-attendance in my life. I got very upset at first. They were letting me down on my big weekend. But then my husband told me to look at things from their point of view. I was asking people I hadn't see for a long time – some of them since graduating – to travel a long way and spend a lot of money on my behalf. So I scrapped my original plans and settled on a meal in an Italian restaurant in my home city. I emailed everyone to tell them my plans and a huge number responded favourably. ❞

Never trust your friends on a hen night

So you trust your friends, do you? You think they know you inside and out, that they appreciate you exactly for what you are: a sophisticated, intelligent modern girl about to take a serious step into life with one man? You think that when it comes to planning your hen night, they will understand that you don't want any strippers, that you never have enjoyed dancing on tables in suburban discotheques and that you have never had a penchant for huge black vibrators that talk as they jiggle. Funny that, because these things just might happen. This may be your hen night but it is their chance to have fun. In a world where women are career-minded, politically correct, and, let's face it girls, doing a lot better than most men out there, the hen night is the perfect excuse to regress to what all women are deep, deep down: drunken, obnoxious, perverted tarts. Am I being unfair? Think about it: how many hen nights have you been on where sticking a condom-covered veil to your betrothed friend has seemed like the most hysterical idea in the world? They are probably organising a knickerless limbo competition for you in your favourite bar as you are reading this.

Learning to grin and 'bare' it

No bride-to-be wants to be a pooper at her own party so try to smile through the embarrassment. It is this basic, courageous instinct that gets us women into so much trouble. To all you past brides who have been made to wander around town centres wearing a disgusting bridal gown and a pair of plastic breasts, my heart goes out to you. You were giving your friends their money's worth. You brave, brave souls.

Hen-night clichés every bride can expect:

◆ L-plates attached to the bride's back and vehicle for the night, although being a learner probably isn't true in this day and age.

- Tampons dipped in red wine, ketchup or other blood-like substances, attached to a veil to enhance the general air of complete grossness.

- A ball and chain around the ankle, to show this girl will soon be a slave to the opposite sex and to trip her up when she gets tipsy.

- Bananas, cucumbers, or a marrow for the ambitious, to initiate comments such as 'Phroaw, what a big one!' throughout the night.

- Strippers, because as we know, what every girl really wants is a sweaty, bulked-up groin shoved in her face and a good gulp of shaving foam.

Finding a fun theme

To make the hen night humiliation a bit more bearable, lots of brides and bridesmaids are coming up with clever themes for such events. This ensures that it's not only the bride that looks ridiculous, her whole posse do too. Here are a few inspired choices from original, party-mad hens.

Cowgirls and red Indians

Costume: dress up *à la* Madonna in stetson and spikes, or become little Pocahontases for the night. Easily available from all good fancy-dress shops. It's also worth looking in your dad's wardrobe, as plaid shirts, knackered jeans and brown leather belts work wonders.

Location: try to book a Tex-Mex for dinner (a curry at the local Tandoori Indian is really getting your themes crossed) and for added hilarity, pretend you are riding horses between stops. Gallop from bar to nightclub – remembering to tie up your horse securely to the bouncer before disappearing, of course. Look to Monty Python's Knights Who Say Nee from the *Monty Python and the Holy Grail* for inspiration.

Props: a studded cowboy hat, an American accent and a whip.

Soundtrack: *Achy Breaky Heart* by Billy Ray Cyrus or anything by Dolly Parton.

Sixties chicks

Costumes: either the Mary Quant mini shift dress or the hip hippie caftan, think Twiggy or Lulu. Raid your mum's wardrobe for this one – or get creative and make your own costumes with bits of fabric from second-hand shops. You can't go wrong with big plastic earrings, a mini skirt and a centre parting.

Location: the best place is probably your parents' lounge. Raid their vinyl collection and talk about free love over a 'few' bottles of Blue Nun. If you want to venture out to a local nightclub, one of the party may have to snog the DJ. He is more keen to play thump-thump dance than Helen Shapiro's *Walking Back to Happiness* but a quick round of tonsil tennis persuades most DJs to change their play lists.

Props: Beatles posters, platform boots and a Mini.

Soundtrack: *Honky Tonk Woman* by The Rolling Stones

Eighties disco

Costumes: come on girls, this is our era. Remember the biggest wedding of all time happened in the eighties. Okay, Charles and Di didn't work out, but they are responsible for spawning a generation of fluffy brides. Dig around and you'll probably find you still have an old Bros or 'Aciiddd' T-shirt lurking in the wardrobe. Add this to fluorescent pink lipstick, pineapple-head ponytails and blue mascara. For added hilarity, add a pair of authentic roller skates and a sweatband.

Location: decorate a hotel suite with old pop posters and dig out your old Brat Pack films like *Pretty in Pink* and *The Breakfast Club*. Or practise your grapevine dance moves in a themed eighties night. They are becoming increasingly popular.

Props: a Rubik's cube and the dance routine to Wham's *Wake Me Up Before You Go-Go*.

Soundtrack: too many to choose from but *Take On Me* by A-ha is a certain crowd pleaser.

The pyjama party

Costumes: forget the fags and booze and opt for 'a night in with the girls' like Sandy, Frenchie and Rizzo. We don't recommend you go shooting down any drainpipes, especially in your nightdress, comfy slippers and silk kimono, but moaning about men instantly takes ten years off you.

Location: your chief bridesmaid's bedroom. Make sure you have access to her back garden. Hallucinatory images of boyfriends past in her paddling pool is a possibility. If she still lives with her parents, bribe them to clear out of your way with cinema tickets.

Props: a face mask, tubs of Häagen-Dazs and a framed picture of the groom.

Soundtrack: music from *Grease*, *Dirty Dancing* and *Pretty Woman*.

Greek or Roman toga party

Costumes: any girl who ever lusted after Russell Crowe in *Gladiator* will know the appeal of this fashion: the simple toga – cheap, easy and very sexy. Also easy to unwrap at the end of a drunken night – for your friends not you. You're getting married, remember? Customise with gold coin jewellery and leather sandals. The bride-to-be could make an effort and dress as Cleopatra, the Queen of Egypt and ruler of the Romans' hearts. Don a black wig and you are sorted.

Location: a Greek taverna or rustic Italian restaurant. They'll think you are weird, but not as weird as the staff at Pizza Hut would.

Props: an astounding knowledge of Greek mythology and a bunch of grapes.

Soundtrack: bazooka music or, if you are really stumped, the music from the film *Spartacus*.

Ladies who lunch

Costumes: live like Jackie and Joan Collins, even if it is only for one day! Dress up in your finest jewels and accessories. Try a showy skirt suit and stilettos. Subtlety isn't important here.

Location: arrange to meet for a late luncheon or afternoon tea at the swishest hotel in town. After a few glasses of champers to wash down the cucumber sandwiches, head to the nearest spa for a relaxing facial and manicure before reconvening in the Jacuzzi to make dinner plans. Then spend the rest of the night visiting the town's celebrity haunts.

Props: all you need to follow this theme through is a healthy bank balance and a sense of style.

Soundtrack: *Diamonds are a Girl's Best Friend* sung by a breathy Marilyn Monroe.

Murder she wrote

Costumes: Murder Mystery Weekends – whether hosted in a private home or in a country house hotel – call for a serious sense of amateur dramatics. Pick an era and fulfil your fancy-dress fantasies. Women become men, tarts become vicars... a few nun costumes should be thrown in for good measure.

Location: either buy one of the many 'host your own murder mystery party' packs or seek out a hotel that offers this as a themed weekend. Local tourist offices and drama groups will have details.

Props: a blood-curdling scream, a pickaxe and a notepad and pen.

Soundtrack: *Thriller* by Michael Jackson or *Somebody's Watching Me* by Rockwell.

NB Also think about horse-races, paint-balling, New Age retreats, karaoke bars, casinos, tenpin bowling allies, seaside fairs, theme parks, clay pigeon shooting, open-air concerts, countryside picnics...

Fun and games

Things to make and do when you're not drinking tequila from a pint glass:

Guess the length of the blow-up doll's penis

The old one's are always the best, and Anne Summers sex shops now sell specialist willy-measuring rulers for such cheeky pursuits. Like a saucy version of the classic summer-fête game – guess how many sweets are in the jar – the nearest guess wins a prize. Try to make it something appropriate: a penis-shaped lollipop always works a treat, as do edible knickers.

Pass the parcel to make you blush

This should be organised by your chief bridesmaid (although it's better if the bride knows nothing about this, so maids of honour, read on). Wrapped between each layer, is a piece of paper containing a question about the bride. They can be as silly or rude as you wish – depending on who is at this party. Questions like, 'Who was the bride's first snog?' or 'What is the bride's most raunchy moment?' always go down well. Embarrassing for the bride, but also a good way of reminiscing about the past and realising what a good deal you've got now. Some of your past relation-ships have been terrible. Correct answers win a prize from a pre-organised lucky dip. Again, (can you sense a theme here?) sexy sweets, such as chocolate nipples, go down well.

Passing the plastic bottle

This game sounds ridiculous. It is. But when I played it on my hen night, we laughed so much we wet ourselves. It's very cheap too. Divide into two teams and lie on the floor. The first two members of the team should place an empty plastic bottle between their feet. The aim is to pass the bottle between all the members of the team only using the feet, and pass it back to the front again, before the other team. It's so funny to see your friends lolling about on the floor with monkey-like legs that you can forget that you are sophisticated laydeez that really should know better.

Pin the tail on the donkey
But we're not talking about just any donkey. Peruse the cheeky mags for a well-endowed, naked man, blindfold your friends and set them forth towards his manhood with a fig-leaf pin.

Twister
A game of Twister, preferably in fancy dress is a must-have for a nutty hen night. Preferably do it when you have returned to your hotel room/house. Bouncers can be terribly difficult about plastic sheets and heaps of girls on dance-floors.

Youth club games
Set out play stations around the room where people can play their favourite childhood games: Kerplunk, Articulate, Guess Who?, Hungry Hippos, Cluedo and Pictionary. Ask all your friends to bring a favourite so there is a good variety and no one will get bored. Divide into teams and set up mini leagues to test each other. The winning group get a bottle of champagne and yes, you guessed it, some sexy sweets.

Should you invite your mother?

Hen nights are a time for truth, tastelessness and debauchery. For the same reason that it might not be wise to invite colleagues – especially if they're higher up the career ladder than you – maybe your mother shouldn't hear about your sexual exploits or the gory details of your relationship. But what if she is desperate to come along? Either hold two hen nights – a tame one and the real one, or brief your friends on what really is acceptable to discuss. People will understand and keep within the barriers – most girls know the shame of a disapproving mother.

Should you invite your mother-in-law?

Your mother-in-law is a different matter. She isn't filled with unconditional love for you but she worships her son. Any sign that he may be marrying a scarlet woman and she'll be on the phone causing trouble straight away, or at least storing information to whisper to the extended family at the wedding. I was lucky. My mother-in-law insisted she wouldn't be able to join us on my 'tame' hen night because she is allergic to sick (what does she think my friends are?) so I was spared any later embarrassment. If you feel she really should be included, sit her with your mother and more sensible friends and warn your friends in advance. The only thing scarier than a disgusted mother is a disgusted mother-in-law.

What if your mother flirts with the stripper?

This might be your mother's first truly mad girl's night for a long, long time. If she does get a little carried away, pinch the waiters' bottoms and start the Macarena from her chair, try to be proud. Hopefully your daughter will be as generous to you one day. It is difficult. However much I drank on my hen night, the sight of my mother sucking her red wine through a plastic penis, kept me sober. But she had the best time and loved being able to meet all my friends before the wedding. Accept that your mother is human and let her enjoy a little flirtation. There's no need to call her a cab until she starts throwing her knickers at the stripper.

Should you invite male friends on your hen night?

This is the 21st century and you probably have as many good male friends as you do female friends. It might seem weird that you are not officially allowed to include some close confidants at your big party, especially if you have some gay friends who you suspect would enjoy the cocktail night at the local discotheque more than your other friends. So ask them if they mind. Most men would probably be horrified at the thought of spending a drunken night with fifteen squealing girlies in fancy dress and be happy to be left out. If they do show an interest in coming, ask your female friends if they mind. A lot of girls can't act the same with a male audience and hen nights are really designed so that everyone can let their hair down.

Don't assume the answer is to invite your male friends to your partner's stag night. Remember: they are your friends, not your partner's, and if he hasn't mentioned it to you it's probably because he doesn't want them there. You wouldn't want your hen night watered down with lots of your fiancé's female friends, would you? If you do end up with a few male party guests, don't change your behaviour to suit them. They know what they are letting themselves in for. They can use the experience as a lesson into the female psyche.

The stag night

So now we know what girls get up to on hen nights. Strippers, dildos, tequila shots and vomiting – and we are supposed to be made of sugar and spice and all things nice. What about the men? In general, stag nights are getting tamer as women get wilder. Sure they still like to drink, dance and leer at a few ladies, but modern man has a penchant for barging, trekking and golfing weekends with their mates – or even 'cultural' city visits (most popular destinations for this are still Dublin and Barcelona).

   Should you panic about your man being taken off by his friends? Well the good news is, it seems female strippers are going out of business. While the ladies are making millionaires of The Chippendales, the humble policewoman-striptease is becoming increasingly redundant. And men won't want this told, but as they are getting more and more dominated by their girlfriends, they're probably too scared to try anything too wild. The two classic stag-night tricks are still hanging about – shaving the groom's eyebrows and/or stripping him and tying him to something in a public place. I returned home from my hen night to see my husband bound up with gaffer tape and secured to our front railings. He didn't seem to mind too much, he was sipping Jack Daniels from a straw through a hole in the tape when I found him, but this was an evil-comic enough event to keep his mates happy. The old trick of getting the groom to a prostitute for his last night of freedom is long gone – they cost too much these days. The best thing to do is hold the hen and stag nights at the same time. That way you'll be so drunk and happy yourself, you won't panic about what he's getting up to on the other side of town.

SARAH, 25

❝ My husband and I decided to hold our hen and stag nights at the same time but we made one huge mistake: we both agreed, whatever happened during the course of the evening, we would meet up at the end of the night at home. Off we went to separate locations at the opposite ends of town. His friends are quite sedate so I thought there would be more wild goings-on at our end. I was wrong. As the taxi pulled into our street, I could see a hunched figure lying on the pavement. It was my husband. He was gaffer taped from top to toe and wrapped around the garden railings. I have never sobered up so fast in my life. Eventually we got him inside to be greeted by about six pissed blokes and a pile of vomit in the kitchen. I wish I had agreed to spend the night at a friends. ❞

Contract of good behaviour

Despite turning into a bunch of lightweights, men are still tempted to drag their betrothed friend along a path of humiliation. Most tricks are immature, pointless and down-right ridiculous in the cold light of day. But to ensure nothing irreversible happens on the stag night, ask the best man to promise you the following:

> *(date)*
>
> *I, the best man at your wedding, will not allow your fiancé to be stripped, dyed, shaved or scarred. I will not give him any love bites that will be seen above his shirt collar, and, at the same time, I will not allow anyone else to do this either, despite how much fun they are having. Despite protestations from the other stags, I will not allow him to be doused in petrol and set fire to. Finally, I promise not to handcuff him, shackle him, or bind him and ship him to a faraway place.*
>
> *He will get to the ceremony on time and in one piece. This is my solemn vow,*
>
> signed, the best man

Secrets of Success

◆ Try to remember that not everyone can afford to spend a for-tune on your hen night, so don't insist on a week in Tenerife or a few days at a Scottish castle when your friends are all struggling to make their mortgage repayments. Also remem-ber that although you think it might be nice to go away for a few days, holiday time is precious (the average holiday entitlement is twenty days per annum) so don't strop out if friends say they can only take part in activities over a week-end.

◆ Don't rely on your bridesmaid entirely. You are the common link so maybe it would be easier if you made the initial arrangements. Set up a joint email list or phone circle for all the girls then everyone can be sure to get all the right information.

◆ Thank all your nearest and dearest by hiding little presents for them either under their pillows in the hotel or on their table place settings at the restaurant. Write a little message on each gift thanking them for their time and friendship. They'll be surprised and thrilled.

◆ Never hold the party too close to the wedding day. Two weeks before is perfect. Allow yourself time to recover from alcohol poisoning, excessive lack of sleep and any skin conditions they could cause. The weekend before the wedding will be busier than you think with final dress fittings, trips to the venue and compiling the final seating plan, so keep it free.

◆ Try to find a middle ground that will suit your quiet, homely friends and your loud, wild friends. Don't insist that everyone goes go-karting, for example. It is your night, so you have the final say, but don't go to any extremes that you know will upset a lot of people.

◆ Designate a sensible friend as your emergency service. She should look after your keys, taxi fair home and your handbag. She should be the one to hold your hair back in the toilets if the thirteenth B-52 doesn't sit well in your stomach. She should also be the one who doesn't ditch you after hours of incoherent rambling about how much you love your future husband, her and the world in general. She doesn't have to be your bridesmaid (she'll be busy planning the evening's entertainment), just a trusted comrade.

◆ Ensure you have picture approval on all snaps taken that night. However funny it was doing *Oops Upside Your Head* with no bra on at the time, the evidence really doesn't have to be waved around at the wedding when you are trying to create an impression of virginal elegance.

Chapter Ten

A speech too far?

EVERYONE LOVES wedding speeches. Well, everyone except the people who are making the speeches, the people who are nervously anticipating a mention in the speech… and beer-loving uncles who would rather get to the bar than sit through hours of sentimental drivel. Women in particular love speeches. Especially pre-menstrual women who see a wedding speech as a high-dosage of classic *Coronation Street* and the last few pages of the *Thorn Birds* rolled into one. Expect lots of tears, swallowing and tissue swapping.

Why do we have speeches?

The speeches give the bride and groom the chance to thank people for coming and for their gifts, and to thank the people that have helped them reach this moment in one piece. The other speeches introduce the bride and groom to their new family and friends and offer inside information in the form of childhood stories or witty anecdotes.

When do we have speeches?

Wedding speeches usually act as an interlude between the formal and informal. Typically, they are announced during coffee, after the meal, and are followed with the cutting of the cake (if you have one) and the first dance, but you can adapt this to suit you. If your speakers are very nervous, why not put them out of their misery early? Hold the speeches before dinner. Ask for trays of champagne or sparkling wine to be taken around as people arrive at the venue, and announce the speeches as soon as everyone has arrived. If your dad is really nervous, he won't mind breaking with tradition. Some people nervously consume so much alcohol during the meal that they are incapable of standing by the time they are supposed to get up and entertain the guests.

Good advice to give your speechmakers

Remind your chosen speechmakers of these simple things and they can't go wrong and embarrass you in front of everyone. The following also applies to you if you decide to stand up and say a few words.

Keep a sense of humour

People don't expect a stand-up routine to the standard of *Saturday Night Live*, but they do expect to see a few funny photographs and hear a few cheeky recollections from the past. You should pick friends who you know will add some fun to the proceedings, and gently remind your dad and fiancé of silly situations you've found yourself in and advise them how to tease the other one.

Keep it clean

Warn the speakers that although the groom may have had a past as chequered as a chessboard, your mother doesn't want to hear about it. And for that matter, neither do you. No blue jokes. No references to the honeymoon, any previous marriages or liaisons, future family or sex.

Keep it short

Ten minutes is the maximum any speech should last for. Any longer than that and you'll hear the gentle hum of snoring from the back of the room and the ruder guests may start to heckle. Try not to repeat the same words or phrases and don't take too long explaining any one event. If it takes longer than a minute for the guests to understand, it can't be that interesting. Ditch it. Do not deviate too much from your planned speech. You might say something silly, boring or plain, old incomprehensible. Remember the old saying, a good speech is like a girl's skirt: long enough to cover the salient points but short enough to be interesting.

Keep away from the booze

A swift glass of Dutch courage is understandable, a bottle of Dutch courage is plain greedy. Speak slowly, clearly and try to stay still. Some speakers sway from side-to-side so much they give the audience seasickness. Others wave their arms around like an air traffic controller. Booze encourages this, so stay sober.

Plan and prepare

The best things for the speaker to do are make notes, time him/herself, practise in front of the mirror and remember construction. A speech should have a beginning, middle and end and shouldn't get lost in the middle. On the day, note key words and names on cards as a prop. A speech read verbatim can seem stilted and insincere.

ANGELA, 28

❛ I kept warning my dad, husband and the best man not to get too drunk before the speeches, but I didn't take my own advice. I was so nervous I downed red wine at the rate of knots and couldn't eat much because my bodice was so tight. By the time they stood up to talk, I was blotto. It didn't dawn on me how embarrassing I was until I saw the wedding video. I constantly heckled, argued loudly over points with my dad and fell on the floor as my toastmaster pulled out my chair for me to accept a toast. So a lesson to all brides: control the overwhelming desire to comment on the speeches. Take any issues up later when you are not being watched by all your friends and family and being filmed for posterity. ❜

Who should make a speech?

Traditionally, the groom, father of the bride and best man make a speech but this can seem a bit man-heavy. If you fancy making a speech, go for it. Or if you feel your chief bridesmaid or mum would like to say a few words, encourage them to do so. Try to plan this before the day though. A chief bridesmaid who gets carried away with emotion (or gin and tonics) and decides to grab the microphone on the spur of the moment may regret it in the morning.

The order of speeches

If you have a toastmaster, he should announce the speeches and silence the room. In the absence of a toastmaster, this responsibility falls to the best man who should then introduce each of all the subsequent speakers.

The father of the bride

When giving his speech, the father of the bride should get the female guests well oiled in the tear department. He should wax lyrical about the love he has for his daughter and his wife (unless his wife is now his ex- and sitting with her new man at the other end of the top table), and he should offer some endearing stories about the bride's childhood. He should perhaps offer a few tips on marriage (unless, as before, he's divorced) and exchange a few corny remarks and glances with the groom along the lines of, 'I haven't lost a daughter so much as gained a son.' The women go wild for this.

While he is talking, the waiting staff should be silently replenishing empty glasses or handing out glasses of champagne (or the cheaper stuff) ready for the first toast, proposed by the father of the bride: 'To the bride and groom.' Everyone should stand and respond except the bride and groom. Get the best man to throw in 'For they are jolly good fellows' or a few hip, hip, hoorays, for good measure, but don't go so far as receiving the bumps. You'll be surprisingly heavy in your dress and you'll look like Dumbo at the circus.

> **NB If your father has passed away** or you do not wish him to make a speech, ask you mother to do so. Or if that is too sensitive, a mature, male member of your family (seems like a contradiction in terms), like an older brother or uncle.

The groom

As soon as the father of the bride has taken his seat, the toastmaster/best man will announce the groom. This will receive the largest cheer from the guests, after all the groom is the hero of the day.

An instant crowd pleaser is to start the speech with the line: 'My wife and I...' It will be the first time anyone will have had you describe yourselves like that, and it sounds romantic, shocking and amazing – all the ingredients needed to have the aunties rushing for the Kleenex. The groom is allowed to plough his own furrow; he can say what he likes, as long as he thanks the father of the bride for his speech and his new mother-in-law for her support. Avoid all but very tame mother-in-law jokes. The audience may love them but they might not make married life very easy. He should also mention his family at this point, welcome those who have travelled a long way to attend and remember those who weren't able to.

The groom should finish by thanking all those who have helped out with the wedding. If friends and relatives have helped you out by making or providing things, show your appreciation with a bottle of champagne each or a personal gift. If the attendants haven't received their gifts yet, call them up to the top table and present them while the toast, 'To the bridesmaids', is declared.

> **NB If the bride, the bride's mother** or the chief bridesmaid want to say a few words, now is the time.

The best man

The best man officially replies to the groom on behalf of the bridesmaids, but the bridesmaids' intentions probably weren't to make the groom squirm. You see, instead of continuing the gentle theme of the previous speeches, the best man is expected to dish the dirt. It is a fine line to tread – too smutty, the women in the group will go mad, too tame and the men in the group will get bored and wander off to the bar. A good idea for the best man is to recapture recent events of the stag night (which hopefully the bride knows about) and to avoid all talk of ex-girlfriends. One-liners work better than a long drawn-out gag. But beware of using the best man speech standards. Last year, I heard seven different best men make the same joke: being asked to be best man is like being asked to sleep with the Queen Mother. It's a great honour but you want somebody else to do it. Boom boom.

The best man should conclude his speech by reading out

any messages or telegrams, making a toast to the lovely couple and running down the programme for the rest of the reception.

JANETTE, 34

❝ We were having a big wedding and our speakers were getting anxious about having to stand up in front of so many people. My dad went to the doctor's for a nerve-calming prescription, our best man went missing a few minutes before he was due to commence proceedings and my husband drank so much during the meal that he ended up making inappropriate comments towards my mother. I'm sure he thought that saying she looked like my sister and his mates all fancied her was meant to be flattering, but she went bright red and I had to kick him hard under the table. If speeches are going to cause this much trouble, go without them. They can be heart-warming and romantic but if you don't think your wedding party are up to the job, don't let them anywhere near a microphone. ❞

Secrets of Success

♦ Make sure everyone who is making a speech has it with them when they arrive at the reception. Perhaps make copies and hand them to a responsible adult in case anyone forgets.

♦ Also, check that no one needs to go to the lavatory before making his or her speech. No one wants to be caught out rearranging him/herself in a cubicle while the toastmaster screeches their name across the room.

◆ If there are more than a hundred guests at your wedding, you will need to have a microphone so those in the cheap seats can hear. A podium or stage of some sort will help maintain interest.

◆ Instead of hiring a professional toastmaster, ask a friend with a deep voice to do the honours. If it will make him/her feel more important, give them a microphone and a gong. Make sure they know what they're doing though (give them a schedule) and don't let them drink too much until their duties are over.

◆ Don't hold the speeches outside if it means everyone standing on gravel (permanent crunching), in the country (sporadic mooing) or next to a busy road (fume inhalation).

◆ Enliven a speech by preparing pamphlets or pictures and asking the ushers or bridesmaids to distribute them to every table. Or hold a mini video or slide show at the front.

◆ Do not feel that you shouldn't have speeches at a second marriage – just change the content. Be a little more serious and leave the childhood anecdotes well alone.

◆ If you are religious, another form of public speaking might be standing up and saying grace before the wedding breakfast. If the traditional version seems too formal for your mixed guest list, try a light-hearted version instead. My dad's rhyme went down very well: 'God of goodness, bless our food. Keep us in a happy mood. Bless the cook and all who serve us. From indigestion, Lord preserve us. If long speeches we must endure, give us first a good liqueur. Amen.'

Chapter Eleven

The judgement day

YOUR WEDDING DAY is going to zip past faster than anything you have ever imagined. Make the most of every minute – even the ones spent on your own – and try to capture every passing emotion. You'll never have another day like it.

Beauty sleep on the eve of the wedding

Nature's beauty fixer is still the most important. To avoid dull skin, dark circles and an attitude problem, try to get a full eight hours' rest the night before the wedding. This may seem impossible, but follow these few easy steps and you're quickly on the way to the land of nod:

◆ Make sure everything that can be done, is done. Nothing should keep you awake (other than pure excitement of course).

◆ Have a warm, aromatherapy bath. This eases away tension and soothes aching muscles.

◆ Rub some stress-relieving massage oils over your body – these will moisturise and promote relaxation. Lavender is great for clearing the head while ylang-ylang promotes deep healing. Then snuggle into your favourite pyjamas and slippers.

◆ Don't eat anything after 8.00 p.m. Instead, enjoy a cup of camomile tea or cocoa to warm you up and wind you down.

◆ Relax with your family and friends, and watch a favourite film or television programme. This should keep your mind clear of the next day's events.

◆ Pray for sunshine.

Morning has broken

You'll wake up on the morning of the wedding torn in two. One part of you will be singing, 'Hooray! It's finally here. No more bloody planning!' And the other part of you will be moaning, 'Oh dear. I've actually got to go ahead and do it all now. Can I be bothered?' By your wedding day, you will have exhausted yourself with the details and arguments; you will have imagined every moment in your head a thousand times and be starting to wonder if it was worth all the effort. Well, wait for it! It is. Prepare to have the best day of your life.

Do you have to spend the morning of the wedding at your parents?

No, the choice is yours, although it would be a shame to be with your fiancé on the morning of the wedding, as this will erode lots of the excitement and adventure. Since the Dark Ages it has been deemed bad luck to see each other before the ceremony (back then, it was so the groom could spend the night praying in the church for forgiveness and strength). If you can't bear the thought of dealing with your parents and your own stress before the ceremony, stay in your home or go to a close friend's. It is a good idea to spend the morning with your attendants though. You can help each other get ready and keep a check on the time.

How to stay calm

Just don't panic. Everything is under control. You've planned everything with precision – and it's too late to worry about things you haven't done. Remember: people love a good wedding, and will attend it looking forward to having fun, to wish the couple well and to get a bit emotional. No one is wishing you ill, unless he's invited a few bitter ex-girlfriends and you've got some twisted cousins. Everyone is determined to make it a success.

If you're still feeling a bit nervous and shaky, try breathing exercises or taking a quiet walk. If you feel it will help, sod the schedule and pop back to bed for a nap. Many people think that alcohol is the answer – it most certainly isn't. A few stiff whiskies might subdue your irrational ranting but drink will also make you feel hot, sweaty, tired and emotional. You'll feel like this at the end of the night. You don't need to start the day like it. Try to surround yourselves with calm, easy-going people. They'll make sure you chill out.

Use this timetable and the suggestions which follow it to plan your day. It is much easier to set it all out than trying to remember everything, especially as the day progresses, and you can give your fiancé a copy as well.

Wedding day timetable

	Time	Notes
4 hours before	_____	_____
	_____	_____
	_____	_____
3 hours before	_____	_____
	_____	_____
	_____	_____
2 hours before	_____	_____
	_____	_____
	_____	_____
1 hour before	_____	_____
	_____	_____
	_____	_____
	_____	_____

	Time	*Notes*
30 minutes before	_____	_____
	_____	_____
	_____	_____
10 minutes before	_____	_____
	_____	_____
	_____	_____
Ceremony	_____	_____
	_____	_____
	_____	_____
Line-up	_____	_____
	_____	_____
	_____	_____
Wedding breakfast	_____	_____
	_____	_____
	_____	_____
Speeches	_____	_____
	_____	_____
	_____	_____
Party	_____	_____
	_____	_____
	_____	_____

Four hours before the wedding

The bride, her parents and attendants should all be getting ready and the flowers should have arrived. The best man is almost ready, so he drives to the bride's house to pick up the fresh flower buttonholes for his party and then goes to meet the groom.

Sound advice: it is important to allocate at least two hours for hair and make-up. If the bride would like to have a relaxing massage, manicure or pedicure, she should have it done the night before.

Three hours before the wedding

The bride's mother rings the reception to make sure everything is all right. The bride is having her hair and make-up done and her attendants are preparing themselves. The bride's mother should be ready by now to help everyone else. The groom is with his parents and best man.

Sound advice: try to eat something around this time. Just a small sandwich or light snack will do but you might not be able to eat again for many hours.

Two hours before the wedding

The groom's party are almost ready and think about heading over to the venue. Arriving early, he can familiarise himself with the room and make sure the tables are okay. He can also drop off the couple's luggage in the hotel room.

Sound advice: many brides and her attendants are tempted to start celebrating early with some bubbly. Restrict yourself to one glass of champagne each – or you could be desperate for the toilet, hot and flushed by the time you get to the service.

One hour before the wedding

The photographer arrives to take pictures of the bride and her attendants before they leave the house. The ushers arrive at the venue and organise seating and parking. The best man rings the bride's father to let him know he and the groom are leaving for the venue.

Sound advice: You should allow 30 minutes for the photographs to be taken. Now is the time for you to have pictures taken on your own, with your parents, your siblings and your attendants as there may not be the chance later.

Half an hour before the wedding

The guests start to arrive and the ushers are in place to hand out orders of service and buttonholes if appropriate. The best man pays the church or registrar's fees. The bridal cars arrive outside the bride's house. First the bride's mother and attendants leave for the venue, followed ten minutes later by the bride and her father.

Sound advice: put your engagement ring on to your other hand. When the wedding bands are exchanged, your left finger needs to be free, and swapping rings over at the altar may get a bit tricky.

Ten minutes before the wedding

If in a church, the bells start to ring and the choir starts to sing. If in a register office, music can be played. Guests should all be seated. The bride arrives and gathers with her attendants outside, while her mother takes her seat at the front. The groom and best man take their places at the top of the aisle, the best man standing on the outside. When the officiators are ready, the bride and her father make their way to join the groom.

Sound advice: your father or escort should take your left arm in his and you should stroll up the aisle together. Catching eye contact with your guests is very special but if you are too shy or overwhelmed, don't worry. Everyone will be looking at your dress anyway. Try to enjoy every moment and not rush through it.

The ceremony

The service will be over quicker than expected. The bride may want to cry, laugh or scream, and secretly, the groom probably feels the same. These are just nervous reactions to being in front of everyone you know. The good thing is, that from now on, you can rely on the people around you (the minister, choir etc.) to make everything go to plan. After all the months of aggravation, it is impossible to believe you are now officially married.

Sound advice: getting married is an overwhelming experience but try to remember that everyone is on your side and everyone wants the service to be perfect. Try to enjoy it – even the scary, official bits like saying your vows. Just remember that it will all be worth it.

The line-up

Despite spending a year sorting out the guest list and the table plan, it's quite overwhelming to see everyone in a room together. The line-up is a fantastic chance for the newly-weds to say hello to everyone. It is a time-consuming process (line-ups can take as long as three hours) so make sure your guests are well watered for their wait. Don't panic if you're not sure who a third of these people are... and even more worryingly, neither does your husband. Your parents will explain later.

Sound advice: don't worry if no one seems to know what to say to you. Line-ups are tricky for all involved so just allow your guests to say 'Congratulations,' and give you a quick kiss before they lunge for the safety of their table. If you can't bear the thought of this flamboyant form of queuing, leave it out. Just make a point of visiting each table to chat to guests during the reception.

The wedding breakfast

Everyone is happily in conversation, and you and your groom may feel a bit ridiculous sitting on a stage between your parents and in-laws. Especially when your friends are getting drunk and balancing the floral arrangements on their head. Now is a good time to do a tour of the room and say hello to a few people and allow them to take your picture.

Sound advice: you may still be too excited to eat, but force something down or you may feel ill later on. Use this time to talk to your new husband about the best bits of the day so far – it may be the only free minutes you get with each other. It is surprising how little the bride and groom get to see of each other on their wedding day.

The speeches

As the speeches should be from five to fifteen minutes each, they should all be completed within an hour. The best man or toastmaster should keep things moving and silence the room when necessary. Make sure there is water on the table for nervous speakers and keep some tissues on the head table for emotional moments.

Sound advice: even if people keep nudging you towards the microphone, only say a few words if you really want to. Otherwise, you'll feel like a fool, and it could ruin your day.

The party

By the evening, the bride and groom should be able to look around the room and see a crowd of dancing, drunken, happy people. If this is the case, they should congratulate themselves on pulling off such a major event. This is the high point… which can be swiftly followed by the low point when the couple realise it is all nearly over. Take the time to speak to as many people as you can, hit the dance-floor with your friends and thank everyone for coming with all your heart.

Sound advice: acknowledge that every trip to the toilet will take you up to half an hour. Not only is it difficult to squeeze yourself and your dress into a cubicle, but also all the ladies will take this opportunity to have a quick feel of the fabric and ask you about everything. You may as well take a drink with you as a light refreshment.

Top ten common disasters and last-minute fixers

1. The florist arrives with the wrong bouquet. Before you throw a fit and refuse to pay her, demand that she returns to the shop and sorts it out. If they can't do this in time, get a responsible adult to ring around all the local florists. When they hear of your dilemma, they will be desperate to help and make it a priority. Ask one of the ushers to pick them up if they can't deliver. If there isn't time, just

select a single rose or orchid and walk down the aisle with that. It will look original and elegant.

2. **The dress doesn't fit.** The easy way to avoid this happening is to try on the dress one week before the big day. That way any alterations can be made without a panic. No bride should be so silly as to buy a dress months in advance and not try it on at regular intervals. If you are particularly stupid and you do have a last-minute squeeze, ask a friend to go to a local department store and buy you girdle pants and tights – they don't look good but they work. If you don't need underwear, remove it to save a few more vital millimetres.

3. **The car is late.** No one sees you in the car apart from your dad anyway, so make your own way to the ceremony with a sympathetic neighbour or guest. In theory, by the time the ceremony has finished, the car will be outside, the driver will be very sheepish – and you will have saved yourself some money. If the car never arrives, hitch a lift with a glamorous-car-owning guest and be grateful this is all that has gone wrong.

4. **The traffic is bad.** This means not only will you be held up, but all your guests as well. Ring the venue and explain the problem. They will normally allow you to postpone the wedding for an hour or so – it's probably a problem for them every day. Speak to the venue about time trouble before the day and warn your guests of any roadworks. Even though it is traditional for the bride to be a little late, don't take any chances. Arrive with time to spare and drive round the block a few times if you have to.

5. **It rains.** What can you do? It's nature. Even the combined force of a super-planner parent and a Bridezilla

couldn't have stopped this. Check that your chauffeur has golf umbrellas to hand to protect your hairdo. To protect your shoes, employ some burly boys to transfer you and your attendants to the dry, or tie carrier bags around your feet with elastic. This trick really works! Just remember to take them off before you go marching up the aisle.

6. You mess up the vows. Don't worry about it. They're over – that's the main thing. It's such a nerve-racking thing to do in front of so many people, that's it's almost expected you'll get a few words wrong.

7. The food is disgusting. You should try to have one meal at the venue before you book it. This will give you a general idea of the standard, although a chef can always have bad days. It goes without saying that often you get what you pay for. If you're holding the reception in a canteen or greasy café, don't expect much. If the food is cold, poorly presented or served in small portions, ask the toastmaster or your father to complain immediately. If it is too late to improve the meal, they can lay on an extra-sumptuous buffet free of charge to make up for it.

8. The DJ is rubbish. Give a play list before the day and insist he stick to it. If he really is awful, the toastmaster can ask for appropriate tapes and CDs to be given to him. Between all the guests' car stereos, you should get a good collection.

9. Someone in the wedding party gets drunk. Don't make excuses. Get them out of the party and into a cab or bed as soon as possible – even if it's yours for the time being. There are too many drink-induced fights at weddings to be funny. If someone gets drunk before their speech, try to sober them up with water and a cold shower if there's

time. Don't give them coffee – all this will do is make the drunk hyperactive.

10. You feel ill. It's not surprising. All the stress, tension and emotion of the last year have come to a head. Even if it's gone better than expected, you can expect a mini-breakdown. Make sure you try to drink water and eat, and give some headache tablets to your mother or chief bridesmaid in case of emergency. If you can, live through it. Your face may ache from smiling and your feet may hurt from dancing, but it's your wedding day and everyone wants a piece of you. You can sleep tomorrow.

What if your families don't get on?

In theory, families put their differences aside at a wedding for the sake of the bride and groom. In reality though, weddings provide the perfect opportunity for a few too many drinks and crossed words. Your parents may not get on with his parents – they might think he is beneath you (common parental belief) or that he doesn't treat you well (another common parental belief). His parents might think your parents are snobs/common/bigoted/ignorant... any number of things. If you are worrying that your parents won't put their differences aside at the wedding, warn them beforehand. Tell them how you feel, that they will ruin your day and that you won't be able to forgive them. This should put them on the straight and artificial narrow.

How to look good in the photographs

Remember your posture and you're halfway there. Not only will standing up straight make you look slimmer and taller, but it will also give you a boost of confidence on a day when everyone is staring at you. Secondly, keep a mini make-up supply somewhere safe so you can get rid of any shine, cover up any spots and add gloss to your lips. A hairbrush and hairspray isn't a bad idea either. Now you look good, how should you pose to capture it? Try to relax – a good photographer should put you at ease – and be natural. Before the wedding, go through favourite photographs of yourself and try to work out your best side, your best features and if you look better smiling with your mouth open or shut. To keep your smile looking fresh, close your eyes and relax between shots and then open again just before the camera clicks. Pictures taken from above will slim the subject (as will standing side on to the camera) and get rid of double chins and wrinkles. Beware of photographers lurking about your feet – this is the most unflattering angle. A bride should not throw her arms in the air or wave maniacally. A glimpse of an armpit will spoil the whole effect forever.

To cut costs, only hire a photographer for an hour to record the ceremony. At the reception, leave a camera on everyone's table to capture the day in their own way. You'll get some hilarious results, including no doubt a few pictures of bare bottoms (it seems to be a new wedding tradition to moon for the bride).

Remember to have a good time

The most common complaint from brides is that the day went too quickly and that they can't remember any of it. It flies by in a flash. Make sure you and your new husband grab a moment together: sneak away somewhere quiet and spy on all your guests. Try to capture the scene in your mind forever – everyone you love, family and friends, drunk and sober, dancing and chatting in one big room. You'll never, ever experience this again – not at Christmas or a birthday – weddings are the one exception to the rule where everybody makes an effort. Then, when you're happy that *everyone* is having fun, share a kiss and tell each other your favourite moment of the day so far, then hit the dance-floor.

Do you have to have sex on your wedding night?

As you leave the party, they'll be lots of nudges and winks. Your bedroom may even have been beautifully decorated with sexy toys and foam. Traditionally, this is the first night that a couple 'make love'. Probably, you've lived together or at least had sex beforehand (under 10 per cent of women are virgins when they get married), so wedding night fumblings aren't such a big deal. Obviously, it would be nice to cement your relationship physically as well as legally, but hey, you've both had a busy day. Don't get too hung up on it if you really haven't got the energy. There's always the rest of your lives for funny business. Surely it's more of a priority to keep your dress on for as long as possible.

Secrets of Success

◆ Lay out your clothes and accessories the night before so that you can have a peaceful night's sleep content that they are all clean and assembled. It is better to put them out of sight though otherwise you won't be able to think of anything else as you drift off.

◆ If you want to put maps or directions in with the invitations, ask someone unfamiliar with the location to try to find it before the wedding day to ensure they are correct. When giving time guidelines, allow for accidents, flat tyres and roadworks. Add a few extra minutes to be on the safe side.

◆ Have more than one board with the table plan displayed or there will be a rugby tackle before the line-up as everyone struggles to see.

◆ If you have any infamous troublemakers in your family, don't invite them and don't feel bad about leaving them out. If they can't behave like an adult, they won't get invited to adult events.

◆ If one of your friends or family shows up with an uninvited guest, try to speak to the caterers and set up an extra place as soon as possible – even if it has to be on a different table. Don't have an argument there and then – it's a waste of your time and you'll only get stressed and it may have been a genuine misunderstanding.

◆ During a religious ceremony, engagement rings must not be worn on the wedding finger. Transfer the ring to the same finger on your other hand before the service. This will save fumbling about or losing the ring, and then you can wear them together straight away afterwards.

◆ If the venue will not allow guests to throw confetti, organise some flower-drying sessions so guests can throw dried petals as an environmentally friendly alternative. Or ask the ushers to hand out pots of bubble mixture for a fairytale scene.

◆ Allow two and a half hours for the wedding breakfast (including speeches) and have the first dance after that. If you are worried about their being a boring gap between the meal and disco, think about hiring some illustrators, magicians or jugglers to entertain the throng.

◆ Think about getting a guest book to pass around the tables during the meal. This provides a nice reminder and gives your friends a chance to tell you what fun they're having.

◆ Even if you have asked for gifts to be ordered from a wedding list, set up a secure area for guests to leave presents at the venue. Ask your mother to be in charge of this – she'll like a good nose – and make sure the gift tags are attached securely so you can send the correct thank-you notes.

◆ If you are worried about guests getting peckish between the meal and buffet, set up a sweet stall in the corner of the room. Visit a warehouse or cash-and-carry and stock up on your favourite chocolate bars at bulk-buy prices.

◆ If you know that your guests aren't into parties, don't drag the disco out too long. It will be better to send everyone off happily at 10.00 p.m. than bored witless at midnight.

◆ If you want to make leaving a special part of the day, think about letting off fireworks as you get into the car. Or be even more adventurous and think about leaving for honeymoon in a helicopter, hot air balloon or on a motorbike. If you fanta-sise about leaving in a vintage car, have a back up. They are famously temperamental on hot days.

◆ Chill a bottle of champagne and put something to eat in the going-away vehicle for when you get to the hotel room, or arrange for this to be left in the hotel room. Chances are you won't have eaten all day and you'll be ravenous.

Chapter Twelve

Learning to accept your big day is over

F OR THE LAST FEW months/years/decades, you have been a one-trick pony. Your trick was weddings and now it's all over what do you do? The biggest thing to remember is that the wedding may be over but the marriage has only just begun. It sounds very sanctimonious but it's very true. You've spent all your energy, emotion and money on planning one big day and it's only after the event that you suddenly think, 'Hang on, that's the party bit over. Now we've got to find and build on a special, new relationship that is going to work. For both of us. Yikes!'

The initial come-down

You open your eyes on your first morning as a married woman. What are you feeling? What do you see? Do you glance over towards your new husband, sleeping peacefully at your side? Do you ruffle his hair, give a gentle smile and think, 'Hooray – I'm finally married'?

Probably not. You're more likely to feel deflated, run-over, upset, and knackered. Well, that's if you are well. If you've got a hangover, you'll feel these things ten-fold. The ex-brides that you'd spoken to in the build-up to your wedding had warned you of this and you didn't believe them. When they said, 'We'd do it all over again if we could,' while staring into their husband's eyes and glazing over, you'd assumed they were mad. Or at least couldn't remember the actual horrors of planning, saving and negotiating their way through a wedding. But you wake up on the day after and you've joined their club. The most fantastic experience of your life is over, it only lasted 24 hours and in theory you can never do it again. The dress that you picked out so carefully is now lying in a mud-stained, wine-sodden heap at the foot of the bed. Your Prince Charming is dribbling into the pillow and snoring loudly. Life is cruel.

The truth about honeymoons

When you are planning a wedding, the honeymoon is the icing on top of the cake. The escapist fantasy for when real pre-wedding life gets too depressing. After hours of flicking through pages of beach hideaways, romantic cities and sexy ski resorts, you will find the perfect place and blow the budget on your dream trip. It will be the holiday of a life-time. Yet rarely will a bride say that the honeymoon was everything she hoped for. Sure there are good points but they can be outweighed by the bad. This is common, so don't think that you are ungrateful when you get to your final destination and sulk.

Positives

◆ You get to relax after all the stress of the wedding

◆ You get away from both sets of your parents (don't leave them the hotel's phone/fax number)

◆ You get to see lots of new, exciting, beautiful things and stay in a hotel.

◆ You get to talk to each other

Negative

◆ What do you talk about?

Your whole life has been consumed by the reception, the dress, and the flowers. Your brain has shrivelled to the size of a sugared almond. You feel that a few drinks might add a little spark but you drank so much on your respective stag and hen nights that you gag at the sight of cocktails. And then it dawns on you both – you've probably never spent so much time alone with each other. You'll think, 'Maybe we haven't got anything to say to each other. Bugger!'

Why are honeymoons disappointing?

There is a lot of pressure on a honeymoon couple to be in permanent mush mode. Honeymoon couples are expected to horseplay in the swimming pool, visit salad bars *à deux* and ignore every other guest in the whole resort. When you are not part of a honeymoon couple, you expect that they are living like love cats, on a permanent heady high of love-making and rapture. If you are the honeymoon couple you know nothing could be further from the truth. If you're in a tropical resort, it's too hot for passion. If you're in a city, you're too busy with a map to stare lovingly into each other's eyes and if you're skiing, well, you're wearing too many clothes to get the coal fires burning.

All the time you're just thinking about the lucky people you left at home. The lucky people who are getting their wedding pictures developed as you lounge by the pool. Or who may even be getting a sneak preview of your official video. And after you and your partner have talked through the wedding day a few times it gets a bit boring. You need new people to confirm that your wedding was the best wedding ever. Why didn't you give your mum the hotel's phone number?

DEBRA, 34

❝ It wasn't until we arrived at our hotel on the first night of our honeymoon, that it dawned on us – we'd never spent longer than three days together without anyone else around. As soon as we realised this we panicked. The first few days were difficult to settle in to. We picked, squabbled and ignored each other. We acted like children. Gradually we calmed down into the pace, shared favourite wedding moments and laughed about the mishaps. It was nice not doing anything and I remembered why I fell in love with him in the first place. Take lots of good books though – it can be tough to begin with. ❞

Where to honeymoon for perfect weather?

JANUARY: turn your life upside down in Australia

FEBRUARY: live *la vida loca* in Mexico

MARCH: safari adventure in Botswana

APRIL: go outdoors in Argentina

MAY: experience *la dolce vita* in Italy

JUNE: high art and high living in New York

JULY: chill out in Morocco

AUGUST: have country flings in Scotland

SEPTEMBER: relax Caribbean style

OCTOBER: enjoy good food and wine in Greece or Cyprus

NOVEMBER: dream away the days in the Canaries

DECEMBER: find island hideaways in the Indian Ocean

Domestic honeymoon

If you can't afford to go away, make your own honeymoon at home. Book a week off work and let paradise come to you. Before the wedding, stock your fridge with your favourite food and get every takeaway menu, buy a collection of fine wines and your favourite cocktail ingredients and treat yourself to your favourite DVDs, magazines and CDs. Book a cleaner to come in on the day of the wedding so that when you return you won't have to do anything. Most importantly, tell everyone you are going away so they'll leave you in peace to relax.

The way forward

A very modern couple I know had their honeymoon before
the wedding. That way, they both got tans and looked great
in the wedding pictures and they both got away from the
stress and drama of the final week. If you can get everything
organised beforehand it might do you good to get away
together, even if it's just for a weekend. You can remind
each other why you are getting married before it's too late.

When do you open your gifts?

Preferably when you are sober. It is incredibly important to
know who got what (people will be asking you who pur-
chased the fondue set for years to come) and to send the
right thank-you letters. Some people will want to see you
open your gift, but mostly they can be stored somewhere
safe by the bridesmaids and ushers for a later date. We
opened ours at about 4.00 a.m., a few hours after the
reception had finished. By this point I had such a bad
headache that my husband had to open them all in silence
and hold them over my head while I was lying down in bed.
I really regret that now. Most brides I have spoken to say
they saved the wedding gifts for when they got back from
honeymoon. It was something to look forward to as they
arrived back to normality.

Thank-you letters

You must send letters to everyone who has sent you a gift, even if you think the gift is awful and have thrown it to the back of the attic never to be seen again. Most people spend a lot of time and hard-earned cash choosing a present for newly-weds so at least pretend to be grateful. A good idea is to write your thank-you letters as the presents arrive (for gifts received before the wedding day). This means you don't have to spend the first six months of married life writing letters.

The easy option: buy the pre-printed thank-you sheets of paper and matching envelopes from a stationer's and add a personal message.

The expensive option: carry through the theme of the wedding and print your thank-you notelets as you are printing your invitations. The gift-bearer will receive the card and automatically be reminded of your great taste and style – and great wedding.

The personal option: pick your favourite wedding picture and make it into cards. People will be delighted to receive a special memento and keep the original card as a souvenir.

The wedding advisor: becoming a stereotype

As soon as you have passed the test and the band of gold is secured, you will become a wedding advisor. Every time you meet a woman who is about to get married, thinking about getting married or fantasising about getting married, you won't be able to resist opening your mouth and showing off, reminiscing or guiding.

You may think you are offering fresh, outstanding advice but you are not. Try to remember when you were planning your big day: did countless robotic ex-brides share their thoughts and regrets with you? Did you wish they'd shut up and let you do it your own way? Try to keep hold of that thought and you shouldn't become too much of a stereo-typical ex-bride. And remember: try to be a good wedding guest. No one likes a goody-two-shoes who says, 'The flowers aren't as seasonal as mine were,' or 'the bridesmaids were a lot better behaved at my wedding'. Let it go. You've got married, you've had your moment. I bet you wished you'd enjoyed it a bit more now, don't you?

How many wedding pictures should you frame?

Hopefully your pictures will be great. Make sure you put some special frames on your wedding list so you can display a few properly. A few. Too many and visitors to your home will think you didn't have a past and you haven't got a future – that you only existed for one day. Alleviate the narcissism by putting up pictures of friends and family at your wedding too – two or three posed shots are quite enough for any house. The same applies for your wedding video. You really should only watch it three times in the first year of marriage or you'll start to suffer from movie star syndrome.

NB It is completely acceptable for grandparents to wall-paper their house in your wedding pictures. As proud grandparents, they are also permitted to make photos into T-shirts, drinks coasters and jigsaw puzzles. Their home is now a shrine to your big day.

The truth about married life

The truth is that not much changes. You'll still argue about him leaving his dirty dishes in the sink. He'll still see your need for a new pair of shoes every weekend as excessive. But the bigger picture does alter to a degree:

◆ You'll argue more because you can. Neither of you can run away very easily.

◆ You'll argue more because you panic. If you don't get his annoying habits sorted now, you could be stuck with them for a further fifty years.

◆ You'll become a family. Other people are still important but the unwritten rule of marriage is that you are working for each other and for your future.

◆ Other people will take you more seriously. Your commitment and love becomes well respected.

◆ Other people will constantly ask you how your relationship has changed. And you'll say, 'The truth is that not much changes.'

Common panic attacks for new brides

◆ You will wake up in the night panicking that you have made a mistake

◆ You will have erotic dreams about ex-boyfriends

◆ You will daydream about ex-boyfriends and panic that you're not over them

◆ You will worry that you are now trapped

◆ You will question your maternal instincts when everyone is questioning you about babies

◆ You will doubt that you are now seen as a person in your own right

◆ You will worry that your husband will die and that you won't be able to cope

◆ You will upset yourself thinking about the reality of divorce

◆ You will exaggerate all the things that could have been done better at your wedding

The reality of divorce

No one can predict the future accurately and no one can predict divorce. Worldwide statistics are rising but you don't have to be one of those figures. You don't know what disaster could hit your marriage; all you can do is prepare yourself as best you can. If your religion allows, live together first to get to know each other's habits. At least go on long holidays together to see how you get on over a period of time. Discuss what you would do if hit by illness, infertility or infidelity. Don't be embarrassed to go to a marriage counsellor or a mutual, trustworthy friend with your questions. Take time out. Do things on your own or with separate groups of people. Try not to become each other's 'other half'.

Common traps for bored new brides

Now that all the excitement, stress and planning for the wedding is over, you need other adventures to occupy your mind.

◆ Moving home

◆ Changing job

- ◆ Getting pregnant
- ◆ Attending evening classes
- ◆ Having an affair
- ◆ Taking over friend's weddings

JANE, 30

❝ I can't explain how deflated I felt after our wedding. I was depressed, bored, tearful. I needed a new project. My husband and I wanted children but he wanted to wait a few years until we had saved some money and moved to the country. Initially I had agreed, but suddenly, pregnancy was the only way I could escape the post-wedding blues. I came off the contraceptive pill on honeymoon, talked my reluctant husband round gradually, and got pregnant three months after the wedding. I loved being pregnant. I got to be the centre of attention again and had something to look forward to. I'm just worried I'll want another one straight away to keep me on this high. ❞

The one-year itch

All of these things could be good for you – except having an affair. Marriage advisors warn that the first year of marriage is the most traumatic and unsteady and these twelve months are breeding grounds for one-night stands and short-term flings. You might feel like an old, married woman. You might feel less attractive than you did when you were single. But if you can't think about your own self-esteem and your partner's heart being broken, think about the guests at your wedding. How disappointed would they be to see what had become of the blushing bride?

Planning the future

The last piece of confetti has flown away and you've posted the final thank-you letter, all that is left now is to plan the future. Unfortunately, no one can tell you how to do this. I can promise you that you will fight, argue, ignore each other and occasionally regret ever getting hitched. But there must be some good points about being married or this expensive piece of paper would have been left behind a long time ago.

On tough days, I think, 'Oh no, I've made a mistake and I'm now stuck with this person for the rest of my life.' On amazing days, I think, 'Oh no, if we die in old age, I've only got another fifty-something years to learn from this amazing man.' The key to happy marriages seems to be learning to accept the rough with the smooth... and trying not to forget the smooth during the rough patches.

The incredible companionship and devotion of marriage was brought home to me six months after my own wedding at an uncle's funeral. As his body was being taken from the chapel to be cremated, his wife of 54 years blew him a kiss, knowing that she would never be in a room with her husband again. She didn't weep, or frown or look away, she blew her true love a kiss. I imagine she had blown him kisses as he left her for the day throughout their years of marriage.

Every couple is unique. Good luck. Enjoy your wedding and enjoy your life together!

Secrets of Success

◆ If you can't afford a honeymoon, at least book the week off work and treat yourself to nice meals out, day trips and a relaxing time. You'll need the time to recover and enjoy your new relationship.

◆ It is romantic when the groom surprises the bride with her honeymoon destination – but don't leave it to him to pack. Also, ask for hints about activities and temperature.

◆ On honeymoon, don't befriend other honeymooners too quickly. This will lead to heated discussions and competitions around the pool and you may not be able to escape them and get any privacy.

◆ Enjoy saying 'my husband and I' and being a Mr and Mrs. Make the most of new events: first married Christmas, first married weekend away, first married dinner party.

◆ As you are writing thank-you letters, write all the correct names and addresses into a new address book. You will never get all these details together so efficiently again as from your invitation list.

◆ Think of original wedding mementoes – not just photos. Perhaps frame your table plan or get your bouquet dried and framed.

◆ Marriage renders all previous wills invalid so this is the perfect time to design new ones. Also think about changing the names on other legal documents like passports and driving licences.

◆ Store useful wedding contacts, articles and phone numbers somewhere safe in case a future bride compliments you on an aspect of your day.

◆ Don't make rash promises about your first anniversary when you are still on a wedding high. Grandparents will remember that you promised to have all the family round for dinner to celebrate even though you've now opted for a romantic night in.

◆ Plan something for a few months after the wedding, even if it's just a trip to the theatre. You need to feel like there's something to look forward to in the near future.

Ideal time planner

Planning your things-to-do list months before the wedding will give you the chance to save, pay deposits and secure your ideal services with minimum panic.

Six months or more before the wedding:

- Arrange the reception
- Choose a caterer
- Book a photographer/videographer
- Choose your flowers
- Draw up the initial guest list
- Order your dress and accessories
- Book your hair, beauty and make-up appointments
- Plan your attendants' outfits
- Ask best man, pageboys, bridesmaids and ushers
- Book church/register office

Four months before the wedding:

- Plan your entertainment
- Book your honeymoon and first night
- If a religious ceremony, visit the officiating ministers
- Confirm your wedding list
- Choose the wedding cake
- Order the wedding rings

- Print invitations and other stationary
- Decide order of service
- Ask friends to perform roles in the service
- Tell officials if you intend to change your name (a passport can take six weeks)
- Book transport to/from service

Two months before the wedding:
- Send out all the invitations
- Buy presents for parents, attendants and each other if necessary
- Visit hairdresser to check style and colour

One month before the wedding:
- Obtain the wedding licence
- Pay off all outstanding wedding debts, if necessary
- Plan hen party and stag night
- Wear-in your shoes at home

Two weeks before the wedding:
- Confirm final details and numbers with suppliers
- Final fittings of all wedding outfits
- Draw up seating plan and write place cards

One week before the wedding:
- Plan your going-away outfit
- Pack for honeymoon
- Hold wedding rehearsal at ceremony venue
- Try on whole outfit including underwear

- Check with florist, caterers and reception venue that they are clear about what you want
- Collect any hired clothes

The day before the wedding:
- Check the venues
- Check the weather reports
- Pack overnight bag for wedding night
- Leave details of honeymoon with a trusted, non-interfering friend
- Speak to all attendants to make sure they are okay

Further reading

Cecil, Camilla, *The 'Harpers and Queen' Party Handbook*, Robson Books, 2000

Chapman, Carole, *Organising Your Second Marriage*, Foulsham, 1994

Chapman, Carole, *Your Wedding Planner*, Foulsham, 1990

Derraugh, Bill & Pat, *Wedding Etiquette*, Foulsham, 1998

ffitch, Dianne, *Teach Yourself Planning A Non-traditional Wedding*, Hodder & Stoughton, 2000

Williams, Christine, *Teach Yourself Planning A Wedding*, Hodder & Stoughton, 2000

Index